Meeting Each Other

by
Daniel J. Meeter

Meeting Each Other
In Doctrine, Liturgy, and Government:
The Bicentennial of the Celebration
of the
Constitution of the
Reformed Church in America

by
Daniel J. Meeter

Wm. B. Eerdmans Publishing Co.
Grand Rapids, Michigan

Copyright © 1993 by Wm. B. Eerdmans Publishing Co.
255 Jefferson Ave. S.E., Grand Rapids, Michigan 49503
All rights reserved

Printed in the United States of America

ISBN 0-8028-0717-8

To Melody,
Servant of the Word

The Historical Series of the Reformed Church in America

This series has been inaugurated by the General Synod of the Reformed Church in America acting through its Commission on History for the purpose of encouraging historical research and providing a medium wherein this knowledge may be shared with the academic community and with members of the denomination in order that a knowledge of the past may contribute to right action in the present.

General Editor

The Rev. Donald J. Bruggink, Ph.D.
Western Theological Seminary

Contents

	Preface	viii
	Foreword	ix
I	Doctrine, Liturgy, and Government	1
II	How Constitutions Work	8
III	Covenants and Constitutions: A Bible Study	18
IV	The History of the Constitution, 1628-1793	31
V	The Constitution: Text and Commentary	46
VI	The History of the Constitution After 1793	145
VII	Three Legs: Interpreting the Constitution	159
VIII	The Constitution in the Future: Some Observations	174
	Endnotes	192
	Scripture Index	206
	General Index	208

Preface

This book was born in Canada. I wrote two of the chapters in the study of the Maranatha Reformed Church of Wainfleet, Ontario. I gave chapter seven as a lecture to the All-Canada Leadership Conference at Camp Shalom in 1990. I wrote most of the book in a cottage on Bob's Lake in eastern Ontario. But I finished the book on a city street in Hoboken, New Jersey. I am very pleased that the book will debut at the General Synod meeting in Vancouver, British Columbia. I have had the Canadian churches very much in mind, and I hope that this book will encourage them.

I did my doctoral work on the children of the first Dutch immigration to North America. My own grandparents, who settled in Paterson, were part of the second immigration. And in Canada I served a congregation that came out of the third immigration. But my warmest experiences of the Reformed church have been the African-American congregation in which I grew up (New Brooklyn), and the Hungarian congregation that was my first charge (South River). I rejoice that what binds us most deeply is not what we look like or where we come from, but what we believe, how we worship, and how we honor each other—in other words, doctrine, liturgy, and order.

I would like to thank Donald Bruggink, Russell Gasero, and John Coakley for all their support and assistance, as well as Henry Van Essen, a "son of encouragement." I thank the staff at Gardner Sage Library for their indulgence. I thank my children, Nick and Anni, for their patience, and above all my wife, Melody, my example and my head.

Daniel J. Meeter
Minister of the Word in Hoboken

viii

Foreword

This volume appears in the year of the 200th anniversary of the publication of the *Constitution* of the Reformed Church in America. But the volume also marks another anniversary, which merits a brief word here: the twenty-fifth anniversary of the Historical Series of the Reformed Church in America. The General Synod of the R.C.A. publishes the series through its Commission on History, and Professor Donald Bruggink of Western Theological Seminary has edited it with distinction from the outset. In twenty-five years, the series has achieved remarkable breadth: it comprises anthologies of sources and collections of essays as well as reference works, biographies, and monographs on a variety of topics from all periods in our church's history. *Meeting Each Other* is the twenty-fourth volume.

What makes Daniel Meeter's study particularly fitting as a twenty-fifth anniversary volume is its clear combination of concern for solid historical research and concern for at least one issue facing the church at this moment; for the principles of good historical work and engagement with the church have underlain the very enterprise of the Historical Series from the beginning. In this respect, *Meeting Each Other* reminds me of the volume that inaugurated the series in 1968, *Ecumenism and the Reformed Church* by Herman Harmelink III. Harmelink's study, like Meeter's, focuses on only a single theme, but by tracing it through the whole of the denomination's history manages to comment significantly on that whole, and most specifically on the moment at which he wrote. In Harmelink's case, his analysis of the long history of controversies over proposed mergers with other denominations hold obvious relevance for a debate that dominated the RCA's agenda at the time he wrote, namely, the debate about the proposal of merger with the Southern Presbyterian church (which was to fail the year after his book was published). He did not neglect to call attention to that relevance in his final chapter; there he made his own position clear (and made his book controversial) without sacrificing good historical method. In Meeter's case, the account of the history of the constitution of the RCA similarly holds relevance for a contemporary issue facing the church and similarly states a clear (and perhaps also controversial) perspective on that issue in the final chapter. This time the issue is that of the denomination's "identity."

The issue of "identity" may lack the kind of immediacy it would have were it linked to a single clear proposal of action before the synod, on the order of a merger proposal; in other words, it may not generate the heat that ecumenical issues raised for the RCA in 1968. Yet the issue is arguably as important. It came to the fore in Leonard Kalkwarf's presidential address to the 1984 General Synod when he posed the question, "What is the glue that holds us together?" An Identity Task Force then engaged the church in wrestling with this question for three years and reported its findings to the 1988 General Synod. The task force's report listed various "affirmations" that one could make about the RCA, identified various "tensions" among these, suggested an array of recommendations and drafted an "identity statement" that has a confessional tone—all of which illustrates that the issue is multifaceted and diffuse, not easily addressed and voted upon. Yet perhaps for that very reason, it remains among the pressing issues before the church. For in the wake of what the report called "a generation of radical changes" in the denomination's organization and demography and in the assumptions and attitudes of its members, the question of identity underlies almost everything we do and is all the more potent for being elusive.

The question of identity will no doubt remain ultimately elusive; the only sure sign that it has been answered will come when it no longer needs to be asked! Yet *Meeting Each Other* offers a very helpful way to think about it,and not incidentally a way to help new members establish a sense of RCA "identity" for themselves. Meeter looks back to our church's history, pointing out that we do indeed have a constitution which (at least in its full dimensions) we had forgotten about, and showing how the notion itself may function as the "glue" of identity even in a situation of otherwise bewildering diversity. This is a similar function to that of the constitutions of the United States and Canada in our respectively diverse nations; and though their success in fulfilling that function is debatable, their importance in attempting it is not.

I hope therefore that readers will view this volume not simply as a history of an interesting aspect of the past of the denomination (in which case they will be learned but few) but also as a guide for all church members, suggesting a way for us to think about ourselves as a church. If it succeeds in helping us do that, then it will be in the very best tradition of this series.

John Coakley
Professor of Church History
New Brunswick Theological Seminary

I
Doctrine, Liturgy, and Government

In the year 1793, the synod of the Reformed Dutch church published a little hardcover book called *The Constitution* which contained three things: the denomination's Doctrinal Standards, its Liturgy, and its Form of Government. This year, 1993, marks *The Constitution*'s bicentennial. Much has changed in 200 years. The Reformed Dutch church has become the Reformed Church in America (RCA), and it is very different from the church it was 200 years ago. *The Constitution* is no longer published as a single, hardcover book. But the Reformed church still has a constitution, and though its contents have been altered and expanded, its basic threefold organization—doctrine, liturgy, government—remains the same. In fact, the constitution continues to be the skeleton that holds the Reformed church together.

The Three Parts of the Constitution
    I.   The Doctrinal Standards
          Ecumenical Creeds: Apostles, Nicene, Athanasian
          Reformed Confessions: Heidelberg Catechism, Belgic
             Confession, Canons of Dort
    II. The Liturgy
    III. The Government, Disciplinary Procedures, and
          Formularies

We in the Reformed church are inclined to take our constitution for granted, but not all churches have such a document. In fact, the two churches which are most closely related to the Reformed church do not have one. The *Nederlandse Hervormde Kerk* (Netherlands Reformed Church) is the "mother" church of the RCA and it has no constitution; neither does the Christian Reformed church, the "sister" which split off from the RCA. Why does the Reformed church have one? Chapter four will seek to answer that question fully, but the short answer is that, even though the RCA was founded in 1628, it became independent of the church in Holland only in the 1780s. This was an era of constitution-making in general, just after the American Revolution. The thirteen colonies had set themselves free from Europe, and to prevent anarchy they had to come up with a new and permanent organization. May of the European institutions within the new America followed suit, including the various churches. So, by 1792, three years after the Philadelphia Convention had finished a constitution for the United States, the synod of the Reformed Dutch Church in North America settled on its own constitution. The next year it was published, in English, not only for the use of the Dutch Reformed church itself, but also as a friendly testimony to the other denominations.

For several decades the Reformed church continued to publish *The Constitution* as a single, hardcover book. (It also continually published another book called the *Psalms and Hymns*, the denominational hymnbook, which always included the Liturgy and the Heidelberg Catechism.) The last complete edition of *The Constitution* appeared in 1879. After that date the various parts of it were printed in separate publications. Today two parts of it, the "Doctrinal Standards" and the "Liturgy," are published together in a loose-leaf called *Liturgy and Confessions*. The other part of it, The "Government," together with the "Disciplinary Procedures" and the Formularies," is published in a loose-leaf called *The Book of Church Order*, known as the *BCO*. But the *BCO* also contains the "By-Laws of General Synod," which is *not* part of the constitution, and this causes some confusion.

Although the constitution is now dispersed among several documents, its basic threefold organization remains intact: doctrine, liturgy, and government. This distinctive shape, like a three-legged milking stool or a three-sided triangle, has given the RCA's constitution its peculiar strength and stability and makes it well worth maintaining. The particular genius of this threefold shape will be explored in chapter seven.

The RCA's constitution is too often misunderstood. For example, several generations of seminary students studied from W.H.S. Demarest's book called *Notes on the Constitution*. This was an excellent book, and old copies are worth keeping, but the very title of the book is misleading. The book does not deal with the whole constitution, but only with the Government, which is but a third of the constitution. Demarest's book has no "notes" at all on the other two-thirds, the Doctrinal Standards and the Liturgy. One still hears many pastors mistakenly equating the constitution with the Government.

It is an easy mistake to make. In the United States and in Canada, where we have national constitutions, we tend to think of any constitution as a set of laws. And it is true that a church must have its laws, since, like a nation, it is a society, with patterns of authority and judgments and the like. A church is also something different from a nation, however. For example, a church has no territory and no borders, but one could say that the territory of a church is the beliefs of its members. In a nation the citizens all share the same piece of the planet, while in a church the members all share the same belief. The beliefs of a church are the very ground on which its members build their lives of faith, so that what a church *believes* is even more constitutional to it than the laws by which it governs itself. So it makes sense that the RCA constitution includes the Doctrinal Standards, in spite of Dr. Demarest's misnomer.

To continue the same point, all the Reformed churches, not only the Dutch one, have shared the conviction that biblical doctrine is even more a "law" for the church than are the rules of church order and government. That is why most Reformed churches (and Lutheran ones as well) have doctrinal standards and confessional documents, and their pastors must "subscribe to" these standards and declare their allegiance to them. The typically Reformed idea is that doctrine is the first priority of a church, and all the rules of organization and practice follow upon this. For example, when it comes to matters of worship, most Reformed denominations (such as the Presbyterians) say some basic things about worship in their doctrinal standards, and then include some liturgical regulations in their church orders.

Other churches take a very different point of view. The Anglican Church of Canada, for example, follows the maxim, *lex orandi lex credendi*, or "the law of praying is the law for believing." The conviction behind this is that belief follows prayer. The idea is to get the liturgy right, and the doctrines and organization will follow. Therefore, what the Canadian Anglican bishops try to enforce among their priests is the careful use of *The Book of Common Prayer* (and *The Book of Alternative Services*) rather than allegiance to any doctrinal standard or subscription to any confessional document.

The Reformed Church in America is unique in that it has included *both* doctrine *and* liturgy in its constitution. It is like all the other Reformed churches in making doctrine the first priority, and it is like all the other Reformed churches in having a few liturgical regulations in its church order. But it is unlike the other Reformed churches in having a full liturgy as part of its constitution. The Liturgy is the third leg of the milking stool. This means, for example, that if a pastor wants to perform a baptism in the RCA, it isn't only the liturgical regulations in the Church Order that she has to satisfy, but the (constitutional) Order for Baptism in the Liturgy. It also means that if anyone wants to find out what baptism means in the RCA, it is not only the Doctrinal Standards that must be consulted, but also the Liturgy. As another example, someone who is thinking of becoming an RCA pastor will find his job description not only in the Church Order, but also in the Doctrinal Standards, and also in the Liturgy's Order for the Ordination of Ministers.

Clearly, the RCA's constitution has a strength and breadth that it would not have if it were only a single kind of document, a legal one, for instance. It is like a rope that is braided from three different strands, or like J.S. Bach's famous chorus from "Sleepers Wake," with its three different voices—basso continuo, soprano obligato, and tenor melody—each with its own distinctive song, moving in counterpoint but yielding a marvelous harmony. The Reformed church's constitution is a trio sonata of doctrine, worship, and government, and that makes it one of the best things about the RCA.

Two hundred years ago the Reformed Dutch Church in North America gave serious thought to its very identity. Even though it was already 150 years old, the new American context demanded that it take a fresh look at itself. In the two centuries that followed, the RCA gradually became less Dutch and more diverse. This diversity is doubtless a good thing, since it is a foretaste of the great diversity of languages and cultures that will inhabit the New Jerusalem. But diversity creates a problem for the RCA, especially since it in no way claims to be the only true church or even the best one. So the question is why people should belong to it, if ethnic reasons no longer count? In the last ten years the denomination has once again been seeking its identity and asking the question, "What is the glue that holds us together?"

If the constitution is not the glue, it is certainly the skeleton. It is the one thing that all Reformed church members have in common, whether they like it or not. Our customs will vary between Schenectady and San Diego, and feelings in Manitoba will differ from those in Manhattan, but in all these places, RCA congregations are equally bound to the constitution. The better our office-bearers know it, the more they'll have in common. The more deeply our pastors and elders understand it, the more loyal they can be to each other and the more joyful will be their working together. And at this point, if it hasn't come through already, I have to declare that I am a fan of the RCA constitution. Not everything in it is of equal excellence, and it may be due for a good pruning, but I believe there is a good deal of wisdom within it, more, even, than the authors themselves might have been aware of. It draws on some twenty centuries of sober Christian experience, and the RCA is fortunate to have it.

This book is meant to help deacons, elders, pastors, seminarians, and church school teachers become more familiar with the constitution. But it is meant to serve other purposes as well. It is meant to celebrate the constitution's bicentennial. It is also meant to be a historical resource, and to make available those parts of the original constitution which have been out of print for almost a century. Certain chapters will be of more interest to some people than others, and not everyone will be equally interested in chapters four and six, which are meant to fill a gap in RCA church history.

Chapter two is a bit of word study and political science in the service of the church. It explains how constitutions work in general. It then compares the ways that various churches are constituted, and how these basic differences have caused the churches to respond in divergent ways to one particular issue. Chapter three is a Bible study which traces the progressive stages in the constitution of the Holy Catholic Church from the covenants of the Old Testament to the apostolic constitution of the New Testament. Chapter four is church history, telling the story of our denomination's constitution through 1793. The chapter quotes a quantity of synodical minutes. These were all written originally in Dutch, but they are quoted here in the official English translations. Chapter five reproduces the full text of sections of the original constitution that have been long out of print. Chapter six picks up our church's history where chapter four left it, telling the story from 1793 until today. Chapter seven is practical theology, explaining how the constitution helps keep us Reformed, how it relates to the Bible, and how the three legs work together. Chapter eight makes some suggestions for how the RCA should keep its constitution fit and trim.

Some definitions are in order. The first leg of the constitution is the Doctrinal Standards. These include the Belgic Confession, the Heidelberg Catechism, and the Canons of the Synod of Dort. Sometimes the Belgic Confession is called the Netherlands Confession. It was originally written in French in 1561. The Heidelberg Catechism, also called the Palatinate Catechism, was written in German in 1563. The Canons of the Synod of Dort were written in Dutch and Latin in 1619.

Sometimes the three Doctrinal Standards are called the Forms of Unity, because they guaranteed the unity of belief, teaching, and preaching of all who subscribed to them. Sometimes the three are called the Confessions of the RCA, the catechism and the canons as well as the Belgic Confession. That is because all three have a confessional nature, that is, all three testify to the world and declare to other churches what the RCA stands for.

The second part of the constitution is the Liturgy. The Liturgy too has a confessional nature. The Standards are what the RCA confesses to the world, while the Liturgy is what the RCA confesses when it is having its meetings with God. The word "liturgy" has been in use among us from our very beginnings in the Reformation era. It comes from a New Testament Greek word, *leitourgia*, meaning "service" or "obligation."[1] In 1793 the Nicene and Athanasian Creeds were included in the Liturgy, but in modern times they've been placed in the Doctrinal Standards. The Apostles Creed is used in the Heidelberg Catechism and in various orders in the Liturgy. Since 1987 the Liturgy has also included a document called the Directory.

The third part of the constitution is the Government. It is sometimes called the Church Order. Appended to it are the Disciplinary Procedures and the Formularies, which provide the official wordings for certain important documents in the ordinary life of the church.

Originally, the constitution also included something in the Doctrinal Standards called the Compendium. This document was an adaptation of the Heidelberg Catechism for children, and it was usually regarded as an appendix to the catechism. It fell out of the constitution without any specific decision to delete it. The same thing happened to a long document called the Consolation of the Sick, which had always been appended to the Liturgy. The version of the Canons of Dort which appeared in the 1793 *Constitution* was considerably shortened by the deletion of the sections called "Rejection of Errors." Taking these sections out made the canons much less obviously antagonistic to other Christians, but some of the best biblical exposition in the canons was also lost.

More than 100 years ago, in 1885, the Classis of New Brunswick overtured the General Synod to prepare a critical edition of the constitution. The General Synod agreed that such an edition was necessary, and a committee was appointed which began the task. Unaccountably, after two years, the committee did not report again. The critical edition was never published. In the last few decades parts of the constitution have appeared in critical editions. Various scholars have published editions of the respective Doctrinal Standards.[2] A critical edition of the Liturgy was finished in 1989 and may eventually be published as part of the RCA Historical Series.[3] The critical edition of the remainder of the constitution is the heart of this book, and so, at last, the job is complete, a fitting birthday present from the Reformed church to itself on the occasion of its constitution's bicentennial.

II

How Constitutions Work

The word *constitution* can be used in different ways. We say, for example, that one person has a healthy constitution and that another has a sickly constitution. By this we mean that the first person seems tougher and stronger and is better able to weather sickness and adversity. The second person may have bigger muscles and be able to lift heavier things and run faster but still seems to get sick quicker and stay sick longer. In this sense of the word, a *constitution* is the total make-up of a human body, its relatively permanent and distinctive physical nature.

Constitutions have to do with bodies. This is true not only of physical bodies, but of other kinds too, such as corporate bodies. A *corporation* is a group of people who have organized themselves legally for a particular purpose. When an organization becomes *incorporated*, it means that, from the point of view of the law, that organization is no longer a group of various individuals but is a single body, a corporate body (the word *corporation* comes from the Latin word for body). Corporations usually have written constitutions, and these are on file with the government. They also have by-laws, the rules of procedure for everyday operations. Corporations can change their by-laws at will, but they cannot change their constitutions without permission from the government, since changing a constitution is changing the very body itself.

Political Constitutions

One kind of corporate body is a *body politic*. Nations and countries and provinces and states are bodies politic, and they too have constitutions. Political constitutions include those laws that are most basic, the laws that are the foundation for all the other laws, the unchanging laws against which all new laws are measured. A political constitution should be relatively unchanging. Because a constitution needs to be valid for many years of changing circumstances, it should not be too detailed nor too specific, or it will need to be amended continuously. So a constitution should be somewhat difficult, although not impossible, to change. And because changing a constitution means changing the body itself, the process for change should require everybody's consultation and lots of time for second thoughts.

Perhaps the most famous political constitution of all is the one that begins with the words, "We the people of the United States of America, in order to form a more perfect union...." This constitution was ratified in 1789 and has served as a model for many other nations in the Western Hemisphere. The U.S. Constitution has worked remarkably well (although some are arguing that it is working less and less well), and it remains relatively unchanged, except for the amendments. Each of the fifty states has its own written constitution, and many of these have been rewritten, some more than once.

Canada has been having troubles with its constitution. For most of its history the British North America Act of 1867 served as Canada's constitution. This act of the British Parliament recognized the confederation of four of its North American colonies into a new political unit, the Dominion of Canada. Only gradually after 1867 did Canada begin to assert itself as a sovereign nation. It was a big step, for example, in the First World War, when the Canadian soldiers fought under their own flag instead of as part of the British Army. Canada increased in size and importance as more British colonies and territories came into it, and finally, with the advent of the British Commonwealth, Canada moved from daughterhood to sisterhood. But as late as the 1970s its constitution was still an act of the British Parliament.

Prime Minister Pierre Trudeau began the campaign to "repatriate the constitution," or to "bring the constitution home." A new constitution was written by Canada itself, and the British Parliament let go of it altogether. There was one wrinkle, however. The new constitution was endorsed by all the Canadian provinces except one, Québec. As of 1993, Québec still hadn't signed it. This means that the Canadian government is operating under a new constitution that hasn't really been ratified yet. Canada has found itself in a continuing "constitutional crisis" that fills the news pages. Canadians have watched with exasperation as their politicians have scrambled over the last decade to find some formula or "constitutional accord" that would "bring Québec in."

This even became a matter of prayer at a recent General Synod of the Reformed church. In 1989, when the Meech Lake Accord was being negotiated, a Canadian delegate to synod led the body in prayer that the accord would succeed and resolve the crisis. As the synod was adjourning, all the news reports suggested that the prayer request would be granted, but only a week later, the whole accord collapsed. In 1992 another plan, the Charlottetown Accord, was drafted, but this was defeated in a public referendum. Canada still has no real constitution.

Formal and Informal Constitutions

It is inconceivable to U.S. citizens that a country can go on without a constitution. But Great Britain has never had one. You will search London in vain for something like a formal constitution. Parliament is free to change any law at any time in any way. Yet, after their own fashion, the British do have a constitution, though it's informal. It is the whole collection of parliamentary law and common law, set fast within British tradition like peanuts in peanut brittle. It's the tradition that holds it all together, and the British feeling for tradition gives their constitution a weight and authority greater than the formal constitutions of many other nations. But a British-style informal constitution cannot succeed in a country with a diversity of ethnic groups, and with people of different histories and traditions. The more diverse the population, or the more cut off from a common tradition, the more important is a formal constitution.

All institutions that last for a long time begin to develop informal constitutions to go with their formal ones. The informal constitution consists of those customs and traditions that are the unwritten laws of an institution. The unwritten laws can be the hardest to change. For example, such ideas as capitalism, free enterprise, individualism, and the melting pot are nowhere written in the U.S. Constitution, but they have become part of America's informal constitution. These unwritten laws have generated the specifically American approaches to such things as education, urban transportation, health care, housing, and agricultural policy. No matter how inefficient or inequitable these might be, they satisfy the deepest conceptions of what America is all about; they satisfy the informal constitution.

To understand fully any nation, or any other organization for that matter, one has to take both constitutions into account, the formal and the informal. When the members of an organization begin with many shared assumptions, shared convictions, a common history, and a common language, when they approach the world in the same way, there is less need to write everything out formally. Everybody just knows how to do things together. But more formality is needed when other kinds of people are brought in or when the organization gets larger or when the organization takes on new jobs and new projects. When things get more complicated, the formal constitution has to be there.

When life gets complicated, we long for the "good old days" when things were simple and people knew their places and their jobs. Simplicity is certainly a virtue, and usually the most simple and straightforward way to do something is the best way. At the same time, Christians have to remember that the Bible begins in a garden and ends in a city. The roles which people may play in a garden are relatively simple, basic, and down-to-earth. But within a city, human activity is complicated, developed, with lots of variety and movement. A city has lots of room (and need) for human creativity and freedom and diversity. So Christians can take a cue from the Bible and not necessarily be afraid of complexity and diversity. In fact, the fear of development and diversity can be disobedience, and that is the message of the Tower of Babel. God certainly wants humanity (politics included) to develop and expand and diversify in a way that is obedient to God's word. And that is no less true with regard to the church.

Ecclesiastical Constitutions

The church is a body, too. There are physical bodies and corporate bodies and bodies politic, and there is the Body of Christ. Indeed, the Body of Christ has aspects of all these other kinds of bodies. It is a physical body (our ascended Lord's) as well as a corporate body (the royal priesthood of believers) as well as a body politic (the new Israel). Since it is a body, it is only natural that the Church has a constitution. The Church's constitution has not been static. It has developed in concert with God's plan of salvation through history. In the next chapter we will look at the constitutional development of the Church as it is revealed to us in scripture.

Within the one Church there are many churches, and they have different constitutions. The Reformed church has a specific collection of documents which it calls its constitution. Some churches (such as the Christian Reformed church) don't have anything they specifically call their constitution, but all of them have something that serves as *constitutional*, whether formal or informal, written or unwritten. Every organization has some basic, foundational assumptions, the set of rules that everyone agrees to function by. Every Christian organization will include some foundational beliefs and behaviors that everyone is expected to abide by. Some are very loose, and some are restrictive. What one church wants written down, another church doesn't. For example, the United Church of Canada requires strict adherence to its written procedures but not to the Apostles Creed.[1] Similarly, the Southern Baptist Convention does not require the Apostles Creed. It also gives wide latitude on matters of procedure, but it does require "rigorous application of funda-mentalist norms," such as the modern doctrine of "biblical inerrancy."[2] The constitutions of the various denominations are the houses they've built for themselves (including the furniture and decorations), where they can live out what they believe.

The Reformed church is a self-consciously constitutional

church. Its consistories and pastors without exception are required to declare periodically that they "remain subordinate" to the constitution.[3] And because the Reformed church confesses, in the words of the Nicene Creed, that it "believes in one holy Catholic and Apostolic Church," it thereby also believes that there is an apostolic constitution which God has given to the Church (see chapter three). The Reformed church is a constitutional church also because it believes that the things which are in the constitution cannot be changed without changing the church itself. For example, it is not so much that the RCA has a Liturgy for Baptism as that the repeated use of a particular liturgy for baptism has continually been giving shape to the RCA. That is why changing the Liturgy is a matter of constitutional amendment. The underlying conviction is that to change the Liturgy for Baptism is to begin to change the church itself.

The Example of Women's Ordination

Sometimes there are conflicts between our formal and informal constitutions. Our unwritten assumptions change over time, while our written documents are static, and our changing assumptions cause us to read our documents differently. One good example of this has been the conflict over the full equality of women in the organization of the church and their right to be ordained to ecclesiastical office. This conflict has taken different courses in the Reformed and Christian Reformed churches, and it illustrates some important constitutional differences between the two closely related denominations. It also illustrates the relationship between formal and informal constitutions.

From the beginning, the RCA Church Order has never used the gender-specific word *males* or *men* in discussing the qualifications of a pastor. It always used the word *persons*. Of course, for 300 years, church members read that word to mean "male persons" only, and our unwritten, informal constitution required that only males be pastors. This reading was reinforced by the fact that in the case of elders and deacons, the Church Order's language did use the gender-specific word *men*.

By the beginning of the twentieth century, however, the status of women in society had begun to change. In the United States, women got the right to vote in 1920 by means of an amendment to the U.S. Constitution. In Canada things went differently and without a constitutional change: each province simply wrote into law the right of women to vote. But women were still excluded from the Canadian Senate. The British North America Act (effectively Canada's constitution) stated that only "persons" could sit in the Senate, and in 1928 the Supreme Court of Canada ruled that "persons" did not include women. Five women appealed the case to the Privy Council in Great Britain. They won, and women were admitted to the Senate. Thus, when it came to questions of women and personhood, the *meaning* of the constitution had changed even though the *letter* of it hadn't.

A very similar series of events happened in the Reformed church.[4] First, in order to admit women to the offices of elder and deacon, the constitution was amended. In other words, General Synod voted to add the words "and women" to the language of the Church Order, and then two-thirds of the classes had to approve it as well, and then the following General Synod had to pass it again. After a number of years of trying, an amendment was approved, in 1972, changing "male members" to "members."

Then, in 1974, the General Synod Executive Committee, in order to preserve the unity of the denomination, recommended that a similar process would have to be followed for admitting women to the ministry of the Word, that "persons" would have to be changed, by constitutional amendment, to "men and women." It judged that because "persons" meant "male persons" when it was written, it had to keep on meaning that now. (The committee must have been unaware of the Canadian experience to have decided this.)

For a number of years the advocates of women's ordination (as the issue was called) followed this strategy without success. Year after year the amendment failed to win the approval of two-thirds of the classes. Then, in 1973, the Classis of Mid-Hudson decided to ignore the prevailing strategy. The classis ordained a woman to the Ministry of the Word, claiming that she was, in fact, a "person." Although many classes submitted overtures to the General Synod requesting that her ordination be nullified, no formal complaint was filed in the proper manner. Her ordination stood, but as an extraordinary case. The leadership of the Reformed church continued to recommend amending the word "persons" to "men and women," and classes continued to deny the amendment the required two-thirds approval.

In 1978, the Classes of Bergen, Brooklyn, New Brunswick, and Raritan all ordained women to the ministry on the basis of the word "person," and several complaints against their actions were filed. The case ultimately reached the General Synod, which is the supreme court of the Reformed church. (The classes and synods are all church courts, or judicatories, as well as being legislative assemblies.) The General Synod had to go into judicial session and decide the case. Just as the British Privy Council had done fifty years earlier, the General Synod ruled that the word "person" should include women as well as men. With this decision, the ordination of women was declared legal in the Reformed church, making the constitutional amendment no longer necessary.

The argumentation in the decision illustrates the difference—and occasional conflict—between the formal and informal constitutions of a church. The Judicial Business Committee noted in its report that it certainly had been the "custom and practice" of the Reformed church to interpret "person" as "male person" when it came to the ministry. ("Custom and practice" belong to the informal constitution.) The committee then asserted this very important principle:

> In a church such as ours, reformed and reforming according to the Word of God, custom and practice cannot take precedence over the declaration of the General Synod regarding the meaning of scripture.[5]

A "declaration regarding the meaning of scripture" had already been made by the General Synod of 1958, which stated there were no clear biblical grounds against the ordination of women to the ministry. With this being the case, and following the principle just stated, the committee judged that the meaning of the word "person" as understood by the custom and practice of the church had to defer to the meaning of the same word as conditioned by the interpretation of the Bible. The committee's judgment was endorsed by the General Synod.

This judgment illustrates the relationship between the Bible and the constitution. The written constitution is how the church puts the Bible into practice. We may say that, for the Reformed church, the formal constitution is the church's bridge between the interpretation of scripture on one side and "custom and practice" on the other. There is traffic across the bridge from both directions, but the traffic coming from one direction—practice—always has to yield the right of way to traffic which is coming from the other direction—the interpretation of scripture.

The issue of women's ordination has worked out quite differently in the Christian Reformed church (CRC). The CRC has evolved a structure that is different from the RCA's. The CRC has no formal constitution. It has an informal one, and it operates more like Great Britain. It has more ethnic unity than the Reformed church and it gives greater weight to tradition, plus it holds to a stricter interpretation of the Doctrinal Standards. At the same time, like the British Parliament, any Christian Reformed synod has the power to revise any part of the Standards and the Church Order. Compared to the Reformed church, radical change in the Christian Reformed church is both less likely to happen and structurally easier to do. There is no process for constitutional amendment, and there is no requirement that two-thirds of the classes have to approve any major change, nor even that the respective classes have to be consulted. A Christian Reformed Synod has more effective power than a Reformed General Synod. The technique that their synods have settled on to retard change and build consensus is the synodical study committee.[6]

Thus, although the CRC Church Order has used the word "men" for all three of the offices, any synod, by a simple majority, could have changed it to "men and women" and opened the offices to all. Since the 1970s the matter has been sent to three successive synodical study committees, each one reporting back that it could find no biblical grounds against the change. Each time, the synod would receive the report but decline to make the change. Eventually the office of deacon was opened to women, but not the other two offices. Then, quite unexpectedly, the synod of 1990 opened all the offices, but delayed the effect of the change until the synod of 1992 could reinforce the decision. The synod of 1992 reversed the decision, however, closing the offices again. But few people in the CRC feel that the issue is really settled, and a future synod may send things back the other way.

The career of this issue in both denominations illustrates the structural differences between them. In the RCA, the classis is really the most important level of government. It enjoys a great deal of the power which the CRC structure has given to its synod, though few RCA classes exercise as much of their power as they might. The RCA structure allows for more diversity among the classes. At the same time, the constitution serves to solidify and steady the RCA like the heavy keel of a boat. It makes the boat much harder to turn, but once a direction is gained, it is more likely to stay on course.

In summary, the word *constitution* refers to the enduring make-up of an organized body. Clubs and societies have constitutions, so do political entities, and so do churches. Constitutions can be written or unwritten, formal or informal, and sometimes both kinds are at work. The way a church is constituted has an effect on how it handles issues and moves forward.

Although there are many parallels between the constitution of the nation and the constitution of the church, there is at least one very important difference. In any modern democracy sovereignty originates from the people. The United States Constitution begins with the words, "We the people." The constitution of Christ's Church begins with the words, "I am the Lord your God," and, "I will build my church." Christ is its Lord and only Head. Whatever power the church possesses is given to it by God. Whatever authority its officers exercise is shared with them by Christ. Even though church officers may be elected by the membership, once they're elected, they represent Christ, and not the wishes of the people. And even though the organizations of a church are devised by human beings, they have to conform to the divine constitution of the church, which is that basic shape that has been *given* to it by our Lord Jesus Christ. How that divine constitution has been revealed to us in scripture is the topic of the next chapter.

III
Covenants and Constitutions:
A Bible Study

The Original Covenants

When was the Church first constituted? When did the Holy Catholic Church begin? Some Christians consider Pentecost to be the "birthday" of the Church. Other Christians believe that the Church existed before Pentecost, that it goes all the way back into the Old Testament. They believe that the children of Israel, the house of Jacob, was the Church itself, but in its Old Testament version. Which one of these do we believe?

It is the official teaching of the Reformed church that "The Holy Catholic Church...has existed from the beginning of the world" (Belgic Confession, 27). That means we must look for its birth not in Pentecost, but in the book of beginnings, in Genesis. This teaching is echoed in Question 43 of the Heidelberg Catechism:

Q. What do you believe concerning the Holy Catholic Church?
A. I believe that the Son of God, by his Spirit and Word,
   out of the entire human race,
       from the beginning of the world to its end,
   gathers, protects, and preserves for himself a community
       chosen for eternal life and united in true faith.
   And of that community I am, and always will be,
       a living member.

This is a wonderful answer, full of hope. It confesses that the

18

Church is most deeply God's work, that God is busy "gathering, protecting, and preserving a community" (or "congregation") by the power of God's Spirit and Word.

At the very beginning of the world, the Holy Catholic Church consisted of just two people, our first parents, in the garden. They had been "gathered" out of clay by God's Spirit and Word, and their relationships with God, with each other, and even with the garden were being "protected and preserved" by the covenant God had made with them. When they broke that covenant God made a new covenant with them, a covenant with a promise. The promise was "the seed of the woman," and though they didn't know it, that seed was finally Christ himself. God was building the church upon the foundation of grace, and God gave it a high tower as a lookout for the promise of salvation.

The Church was first constituted in the form of a family. It continued in that form over many generations, through all the book of Genesis, through Noah's family down to Abraham's family. With Abraham God made a new covenant with new promises: the promised land, the promise of countless descendants, and the promise that out of his seed all the families of the earth would bless themselves. Over the next 400 years or so the Church divided itself into twelve tribes and multiplied greatly, but it continued to be constituted as a family. These are family terms: the house of Jacob and the children of Israel.

It was at Mount Sinai that God brought the Church into the next stage of its constitutional development. The huge family passed into nationhood, it became "a priestly kingdom and a holy nation" (Exodus 19:6), with God for its ruler. The covenant that God ratified at Sinai is about as straightforward a national constitution as there ever has been. (Could it be that Israel was the first nation in history to have gotten started with a formal, written constitution?) The Sinai covenant included elements of doctrine and teaching, patterns of ritual and worship, and structures of law and order. The Sinai covenant gave the forms and patterns by which the Church would organize itself, maintain itself, discipline itself, be recognized, and perform its service to the world. The Sinai constitution had a double purpose: to reveal to the world God's will and God's personality, and to provide a real and workable civil society that would fully honor a holy God and provide justice and peace for every citizen.

The next stage in the development was the covenant with David. The Sinai constitution was still in effect, but God added some "amendments" in the form of new promises to King David's dynasty. The Temple in Jerusalem was the symbol of these promises—the house of God for the house of David. These promises and their symbol became an irrevocable part of the organization of the Old Testament Church. This constitutional development came to be repudiated by the ten northern tribes, and eventually they were lost to the covenant as a whole. But in the tribe of Judah, the Davidic covenant was regarded as harmonizing with the Sinai covenant. The Judean prophets envisioned a day when there would come a ruler from the house of David who would lead the people in fulfilling all the laws of Moses.

The New Covenant

The vision of the prophets, we believe, was fulfilled in Jesus Christ. But the prophets might not have expected that the coming of God's self in Jesus Christ would bring about the total reconstitution of the Church. After having been constituted as a family, as a nation, and then as a political dynasty, God's people became for the first time in Christ that peculiar kind of organization which we call "church." It gave up its special claim on the Promised Land in order to claim the whole world. And whereas the promise of salvation had always been its tower, now the fulfillment of salvation was its very foundation, in the person of the Savior. In reconstituting the church the Lord Jesus enacted a "new covenant" in his blood. Once he had ratified that covenant upon the cross, immediately upon his resurrection he began to invite other people to join him in the new covenant, such as at Emmaus, when, after he had broken the scriptures to them, he met them in the breaking of the bread. His Word became the new Sinai and the Table became the new Temple.

His disciples were slow to understand the total reconstitution of the Church. They were still thinking of family and nation when, at Christ's ascension, they asked him, "Lord, will you at this time restore the kingdom to Israel?" But ten days later, when the Holy Spirit came upon them at Pentecost (the very day when all the pilgrims in Jerusalem were commemorating the giving of the Sinai covenant), the disciples began to get the point. On that day, a whole new people of God began, as the catechism says, to be "gathered, protected, and preserved by God's Spirit (in the fire) and Word (from the rooftops)." On that day in Jerusalem, 3,000 Jews became the nucleus of the Church. That these 3,000 responded illustrates the continuity between the old and new constitutions—the one led directly to the other. But it also shows the discontinuity between them—the 3,000 had to repent and be baptized. In other words, throughout the ages there has only ever been one Church, but God has led it through a progression of covenants, or constitutions, and at each new stage the people of God must respond in faith to God's new deed.

The basic structure of the reconstituted Church was apparent already at Pentecost. We read of it in Acts 2:41-42:

> So those who received his *word* were *baptized*, and there were added that day about three thousand souls. And they devoted themselves to the *apostles' teaching* and *fellowship*, to the *breaking of bread* and the *prayers* [italics mine].

From this we learn that the apostolic Church was constituted by the following elements:

1. The apostles' word (preaching and testimony)
2. Baptism
3. The apostles' teaching (doctrine)
4. The apostles' fellowship (government)
5. Breaking of bread (Communion)
6. The prayers

These elements began to replace the elements of the Sinai covenant which had constituted the Church in the Old Testament.

A few days after Pentecost, when Peter stood before the chief priests of Israel, he testified that Jesus Christ was "the stone which was rejected by you builders, but which has become the head of the corner" (Acts 4:11). He was quoting from Psalm 118, the hymn which the pilgrims had been singing on Palm Sunday at the gates of Jerusalem. In other words, what was going on around them was the rebuilding of the spiritual Jerusalem on the new cornerstone of Jesus Christ. The apostles surely nurtured some hope that the whole of Israel would accept their new constitution. They displayed their loyalty to the temple by continually returning to it and ministering from within it (Acts 5:12, 21, 6:42). This is another example of the continuity between the various stages of the covenantal history of God's people.

Whatever hopes they might have had did not last long. The arrest of Stephen signaled the ultimate discontinuity between the new constitution and the old, which continues to this day as Judaism. Stephen saw that the triumphal entry into the temple which is celebrated in Psalm 118 had been fulfilled with Jesus' triumphal entry into heaven. Stephen saw this when he gazed into heaven at the end of the testimony that cost him his life (Acts 7:55). His vision, when taken with his quotation from Isaiah 66:1-2, "the Most High does not dwell in houses made with hands," implied the inevitable repudiation of the temple in Jerusalem, which was the symbol of the old national covenant. It implied the total reconstitution of Israel. The Sanhedrin understood the implications very well, as manifested by their violent response to Stephen and by the subsequent persecution (Acts 8:1). The persecution forced the church to scatter away from Jerusalem, but this was also the beginning of its mission to the ends of the earth (Acts 11:19-21).

The next thing that the Book of Acts reports to us is the Apostle Philip's mission to Samaria (Acts 8:4-25). The Samaritans claimed to worship the God of Abraham and to follow the prophet Moses, but they had never honored the temple or Jerusalem (John 4:20). They were the descendants of gentiles who had interbred with the remnants of the northern kingdom, that is, the ten tribes which had repudiated the covenant with the house of David. We read that the Samaritans eagerly accepted the gospel. Their disloyalty to the temple in Jerusalem was apparently not a problem for the apostles. We see that the Samaritans, by virtue of their belief in the Son of David, were being restored to the house of Jacob. The kindred peoples that had rejected each other were being reconciled. We can apply to them what the apostle Paul wrote much later to the Ephesians:

> So then, you are no longer strangers and aliens, but you are citizens with the saints and also members of the household of God, built upon the foundation of the apostles and prophets, with Christ Jesus himself as the cornerstone. In him the whole structure is joined together and grows into a holy temple in the Lord; in whom you also are built together for a dwelling place for God in the Spirit (Ephesians 2:19-22).

The reconstitution of Israel meant that the Church itself, as the "household of God," had become the new temple, the "dwelling place for God." If the Church is the Body of Christ (Ephesians 1:23), and if Christ called his own body the temple (John 2:21), then both are true, that Christ himself is the heavenly temple, and that the people of God are the temple in the world.

Directly after the mission to the Samaritans, we are told of the conversion of the Ethiopian eunuch (Acts 8:26-39). God-fearer that he was, he would have been excluded from the temple because he was a gentile, but more serious than that, according to the law of Moses, his physical condition was cause for him to be rejected from the congregation of Israel (Deuteronomy 23:1).[1] His condition must have been very much on his mind when he said, "Look, here is water, what is to prevent me from being baptized?" When Philip baptized him, the apostle was declaring that even the ritually unclean would no longer be rejected from the people of God, and that in the new temple that was being built, the court of the gentiles would no longer be a separate place. As the apostle Peter wrote much later in his First Epistle:

> Come to him, a living stone, though rejected by mortals yet chosen and precious in God's sight, and like living stones, let yourselves be built into a spiritual house, to be a holy priesthood, to offer spiritual sacrifices acceptable to God through Jesus Christ. For it stands in scripture: "See, I am laying in Zion a stone, a cornerstone chosen and precious, and whoever believes in him will not be put to shame." (1 Peter 2:4-6).

The shame of the eunuch would no longer prevent him from being incorporated into God's house as a living stone, resting on the new foundation of the Christ who was also "rejected and cut off."

The Holy Spirit was moving very fast, and Philip was moving with it. It took a little longer for some of the others to catch up. God's dealings with the Italian centurion Cornelius persuaded the apostle Peter to admit Gentiles to baptism without their also becoming Jews (Acts 10).[2] The next stage in the opening up of Israel was the commissioning of Paul and Barnabas (Acts 11) to preach to Jews and gentiles equally. This implied that God was now extending to all believing gentiles the special vocation given to Israel in the Sinai Covenant, to be a "priestly kingdom and a holy nation" (Exodus 19:6). This too Peter wrote of in the First Epistle:

> But you are a chosen race, a royal priesthood, a holy nation, God's own people, that you may proclaim the mighty acts of him who called you out of darkness into his marvelous light. Once you were not a people, but now you are God's people; once you had not received mercy, but now you have received mercy (1 Peter 2:9-10).

The Church had been extended to the whole family of Adam and Eve. In the words of the catechism, "the Son of God, by his Spirit and Word, out of the entire human race,...was gathering, protecting, and preserving a community chosen for eternal life and united in true faith."

The Apostolic Constitution

Already before his passion Jesus had taught his disciples how the church must be constituted. It was at Caesarea Philippi, and we read of it in Matthew 16:15-19:

> He said to them, "But who do you say that I am?" Simon Peter replied, "You are the Christ, the Son of the Living God." And Jesus answered him, "Blessed are you, Simon

> BarJona. For flesh and blood has not revealed this to you, but my Father who is in heaven. And I tell you, you are Peter, and on this rock I will build my church, and the gates of Hades shall not prevail against it. I will give you the keys of the kingdom of heaven, and whatever you bind on earth shall be bound in heaven, and whatever you loose on earth shall be loosed in heaven."

This passage, which can be called the apostolic constitution of the church, provides the basic blueprint which every succeeding generation must maintain. It shows how Christ, though he himself is the "only foundation that can be laid" (1 Corinthians 3:11), immediately incorporated other persons into his foundation. The twelve apostles themselves became a part of the new foundation, as John was shown in his final vision (Revelation 21:14).

To say that the living person of Christ is the foundation of the church is to say that the church is first of all not an organization but a people. In the Matthew passage, the "rock" that Christ would build upon was a person, it was Peter.[3] Peter was a believer, but more than that he was a confessor, one who confessed his faith and testified to the truth of Jesus Christ. Such persons as Peter were the "living stones" with which Christ would build his church. Christ gave to Peter the special position as leader of the apostles, and the apostles were the stones that were built into the foundation. Christ had chosen these specific people to be his colleagues in the work of "gathering, protecting, and preserving a community chosen for eternal life." Through their very down-to-earth personalities, Christ would mediate his Word and Spirit to cause the church to be "united in true faith." Christ was also calling every succeeding generation of believing persons to be in fellowship and community with these apostles and to be united with them in true faith. In this sense the church's most fundamental constitution is personal, unwritten, and "informal" (see chapter two).

But because the church is a people, it must also be an organization.[4] In the organizational sense, it was Simon Peter's confession that was the bedrock of the church. Not only did Peter's apostolicity lay in who he was, it also lay in what he did. He testified to the identity of Jesus Christ; he bore witness in the courtroom of the world. This was true for the other disciples as well, for they came to share in Peter's confession, and our Lord confirmed their apostolicity at his ascension when he said, "And you shall be my witnesses in Jerusalem and in all Judea and Samaria and to the ends of the earth" (Acts 1:8). The apostolic constitution of the church is based on the apostolic confession, and that must be true for the church in every succeeding generation. It is through the written testimony of these divinely appointed "ambassadors" that "God makes his appeal to us" (2 Corinthians 5:20).

At Caesarea Philippi Jesus spoke of the "keys of the kingdom" and of "binding and loosing." Here our Lord was teaching us that the apostolic testimony included apostolic authority. When he breathed on them in the upper room (John 20:22), he gave them a share of his own Spirit to support their authority, even to the extent that they could share in the divine act of forgiving sins. Having authority meant that they would do more than play back Jesus' words like tape recorders; they would set Jesus' words to their own music and perform that music with their own voices. Having authority also meant that they had the responsibility to decide how Jesus' words should *not* be sung. When Jesus told them, "Teach them to obey everything that I have commanded you" (Matthew 28:20), he was authorizing them not only to transmit his teaching, but also to interpret and apply that teaching to specific situations, and to make decisions that would either "bind or loosen" their fellow believers. (Peter's healing of the crippled beggar in Acts 3:6 was an example of "loosening," and his judgment on Ananias and Sapphira in Acts 5 was an example of "binding.") The singular office of the apostles was intended by Christ to have an unchanging constitutional importance for every succeeding generation of the church.

What Jesus said at Caesarea Philippi was a prophecy that came true on Pentecost. By the power of the Spirit, Christ was able to build the church upon the foundation of the apostles' testimony, especially the testimony of Peter, whose sermon is recorded for us in Acts 2. In that sermon, after he exhorted the multitude to repent, to be baptized, and to save themselves from their crooked generation, Peter declared that the promise was to them and to

their children. In doing this, Peter was performing the apostolic
ministry of using "the keys" to "bind and loosen."5

The office of apostle was unique to the first generation of the
church, the generation of eyewitnesses to Christ, all of whom
Christ had selected personally. Paul felt justified in claiming the
office only because of his own direct, divine appointment (Galatians 1:1, 1 Corinthians 15:3-10). The apostolic constitution could
survive the eventual death of all the apostles because, as Paul
taught, along with the apostolate and related to it, God gave other
offices to the church:

> The gifts [Christ] gave were that some would be apostles,
> some prophets, some evangelists, some pastors and
> teachers, to equip the saints for the work of ministry, for
> building up the body of Christ (Ephesians 4:11-12).

To some degree, the authority of the apostles could be maintained
by the ministry of these other persons. It was for this reason that
Paul took great care in choosing the pastors and teachers of all his
congregations. They would have to maintain the very same
testimony and confession which the apostles had handed to them.
They would do this by gathering the authoritative writings of the
apostles—the New Testament. Whenever succeeding generations
of pastors and teachers faithfully maintained the testimony,
"binding and loosing" according to the teaching, even though they
themselves were not apostles, they were building upon the
"foundation of the prophets and apostles," they were maintaining
the apostolic constitution.

This conviction guided the development of the church in the
first centuries after Christ. Some time around A.D. 155, Justin
Martyr reported that when Christians gathered for worship, "The
memoirs of the apostles or the writings of the prophets are read as
long as time permits."6 A few decades later, Irenaus of Lyon, in
refuting the Gnostics, wrote as follows:

> True knowledge is the doctrine of the apostles, and the
> ancient constitution of the church throughout all the
> world, and the distinctive manifestation of the body of
> Christ according to the successions of the bishops,...and a

lawful and diligent exposition in harmony with the Scriptures,...and the pre-eminent gift of love....7

The early church was concerned to demonstrate its connection
with the apostles.

This concern is apparent in the very names of some of the documents that have come down to us from that time. One of the
oldest, also from the middle of the second century, is the so-
called *Didache*, the "Teaching of the Twelve Apostles."8 In the
early third century Hippolytus outlined what he saw as the
orthodox teaching and practice of the congregation in Rome in a
document called *The Apostolic Tradition.*9 This document is
essentially what we have been calling a "constitution," containing
teaching in doctrine, patterns for liturgy, and rules of church
order. Later in the same century came the anonymous document
we know as the *Didascalia Apostolorum*, which incorporates some
of Hippolytus's material.10 This too is a "church order." The next
century saw the appearance of another such document, also
anonymous, called the *Apostolic Constitutions.*11 The first six
books of this document are based on the *Didascalia*, and the
seventh begins with the *Didache.*12 All these documents were
written from the point of view that for the church to be truly
"catholic" it had to be united, across time, with the church of the
apostles, as "One Holy Catholic and Apostolic Church."

The Roman Catholic church gradually developed out of such
constitutions as these, and it can legitimately claim a direct
historical connection with these apostolic constitutions, even if, in
our view, it has developed *away* from them. Such a denomination
as the Reformed Church in America does not have its own direct
and historical connection to the early church; we are connected to
it only by way of our descent from the Roman Catholic church.
The conviction of the Reformation was that the very Roman
church which was the link to the Apostolic church was also the
great obstacle which got in the way of those who wished to be in
fellowship with the apostles and their teaching.

The wing of the Reformation which produced the Reformed
church did not see itself as "reconstituting" the church. They
regarded their activity more like a thoroughgoing housecleaning.
John Calvin, for one, did not want to start a new church or a new

way of organizing the church. He simply wanted to restore the church to its primitive constitution. Neither did he try, however, to restore the church to some pure New Testament practice. He was not a biblicist. His model was the whole primitive church, including the Church Fathers and martyrs, such as Justin and Irenaeus, as well as the New Testament.[13] His earliest manual of worship, for example, bore the subtitle, "According to the Custom of the Ancient Church."[14] At the same time, in discussing the whole matter of church constitutions, Calvin wrote that it was not necessary for the church to slavishly follow the patterns of the ancient church in order to remain apostolic, because God

> did not will in outward discipline and ceremonies to pre-
> scribe in detail what we ought to do (because he foresaw
> that this depended upon the state of the times, and he did
> not deem one form suitable for all ages), here we must
> take refuge in those general rules which he has given, that
> whatever the necessity of the church will require for
> order and decorum should be tested against these. Lastly,
> because he has taught nothing specifically, and because
> these things are not necessary to salvation, for the
> upbuilding of the church [the disciplines and ceremonies]
> ought to be variously accommodated to the customs of
> each nation and age.... [15]

Calvin meant that it is possible for various churches to show considerable variety in matters of discipline and ceremony and still all be founded upon a single foundation.

Calvin's teaching also means that it is possible for such a denomination as the Reformed church to consider itself built upon the "foundation of the prophets and apostles," in spite of the fact that the great bulk of its actual constitution is material that was written so many centuries after the apostolic age. Indeed, following Calvin's thinking, the modern material is necessary exactly for the purpose of keeping the modern church true to "the general rules" which scripture has revealed as being permanently binding, which we have been calling the apostolic constitution:

> So those who received his word were baptized, and there

were added that day about three thousand souls. And they
devoted themselves to the apostles' teaching and
fellowship, to the breaking of bread and the prayers.

IV

The History of the
Constitution, 1628-1793

    The Dutch Reformed church was founded in North America in 1628, when a consistory was established in Manhattan. For the first 150 years of its existence it was a branch of the state church of the Netherlands. For the initial forty years, while New Netherland was a Dutch colony, it was the only legal church, though others were tolerated. It had the exclusive right to be incorporated, to own property, to run a school, and to receive revenues from the government to support its salaries and building (the offerings of the people were given to the poor by the deacons). All this was the ordinary European practice of the time. Each nation had an "established" church to which all normal citizens were expected to belong. The law of the land prescribed how these churches should be organized, what doctrines they should teach, and what liturgy they should follow.[1]

    During the 150 years of the colonial era, all the Dutch Reformed congregations in North America were subject to the Classis of Amsterdam. Because the Classis of Amsterdam was established by the civil laws of the Province of North Holland, we can say that the constitution of the Dutch Reformed Church in North America was still in the Netherlands (just as for the first century of Canada's existence its constitution, the British North America Act, was still in Great Britain). The laws of the Province of North Holland required the North American congregations to conform to the regulations of the famous Synod of Dort, which had met in 1619. They had to organize according to the Church Order of Dort.[2] All the pastors had to subscribe to the *Formulae of*

Concord: the Belgic Confession, the Heidelberg Catechism, and the Canons of Dort.[3] The Church Order prescribed the strict use of the Liturgy and the metrical Psalter.

Later on, the Dutch in America came to call this totality the "Netherlandish Constitution," though it was never published as such in Europe.[4] So when Dominé Jonas Michaelius and his consistory began regular services in 1628, they certainly didn't regard themselves as founding a new branch of the Dutch Reformed church. They were simply organizing, worshiping, preaching, and teaching in the way that the Dutch laws required. This was the way of established churches.

When the English took over New Netherland in 1664, the Anglican church replaced the Dutch Reformed church as the established one.[5] But the English conceded freedom of worship to the Dutch population in their new colony (divided and renamed New York and New Jersey), and even more, they guaranteed that the Dutch Reformed church might continue to enjoy many of the rights of establishment alongside the Anglican church. This status continued for the next century of British colonial rule, and no other denominations were allowed a share of the church tax, nor could their congregations incorporate with the right to own property, not even the Presbyterians, who could claim connection with the established Church of Scotland.

This special status had nothing to do with any English sympathy for Dutch doctrine or worship. The Church of England had small reputation for toleration of other churches, especially Calvinist ones. It was a purely political arrangement. From the English point of view, because the fledgling Dutch Reformed Church in North America was a branch of the state church of another European nation, its special status was really a matter of international diplomacy between two sovereign colonial powers. As long as its Dutch-language worship did not compete with Anglican worship, and as long as it adhered to Dutch law, it was tolerable, even useful, to the English colonial regime. The British governors even granted royal charters to a number of Dutch congregations.

The possession of these royal charters was a mixed blessing, however. The New York City Consistory, for example, which possessed one, was afraid to introduce worship in the English language, for fear of angering the Anglican establishment into revoking their special privileges. As a result, by the 1750s, when the English language had finally become the common tongue of Manhattan, the New York City church began to lose some of its younger families. Of course, there remained many country districts in New York and New Jersey where English was only the second language, and where the inhabitants of Dutch descent, now settled for five generations, were only reluctant subjects of the British crown, just as they would be later in South Africa, or as were the French in Québec.

The relationship between the Classis of Amsterdam and the North American congregations was never a convenient one. Communications were slow, and pastors, who were required to be university graduates and ordained in Europe, were hard to get. (Several pastors and candidates perished in making the sea crossing.) The increasingly restrictive mercantile policies of England made communications with the Netherlands tricky. And as the colonies began to develop their own distinctively American culture, the Classis of Amsterdam grew even less sympathetic to colonial needs than it had been. When North American conditions made adhering strictly to Dutch procedures increasingly difficult, the Dutch church split between the *Coetus* and *Conferentie* parties. The Coetus advocated some independence from the classis, especially the right to educate and ordain its own pastors. The Conferentie stood by the status quo.[6] The Coetus and Conferentie schism, which lasted a whole generation, is one of the saddest chapters of our history and doubtless stunted the growth of the Reformed church at an important stage of its life.

In spite of the Coetus's desire for greater independence, it was just as loyal to the distinctive constitution of the church as the Conferentie was. The "Fundamental Articles" by which the Coetus had been organized in 1738 clearly expressed fidelity to "the Constitution of our Church as established in the Synod of Dort."[7] Although many members of the Coetus began to depart from the articles in practice, their demands for independence were never more extreme than requesting the right to organize a North American Classis within the Particular Synod of North Holland. The constitution itself would have been maintained.

Finally, in 1768, with the assistance of the young John Henry

Livingston, who was studying at the University of Utrecht, the Classis of Amsterdam took steps to put an end to the schism. The classis drafted a Plan of Union, which Livingston carried to New York and distributed to both the Coetus and the Conferentie. In October of 1771, the New York consistory was able to host a union convention at which both parties were present. A Formula of Union was drafted, the first article of which stated, "We adhere, in all things, to the constitution of the Netherlands Reformed Church, as the same was established in the church orders of the Synod of Dordrecht, in the years 1618 and 1619."[8]

The Plan of Union was sent back to the Netherlands, and in January, 1772, it received the approval of Classis Amsterdam.[9] In June of that year a second Union Convention endorsed it again.[10] The long-sought-for rights of education and ordination were granted. The church was allowed to organize itself into a General Assembly and several particular assemblies, although the terms *Synod* and *Classis* were avoided out of deference to the Synod of North Holland and the Classis of Amsterdam. These still reserved the right to hear all appeals. But by means of the 1771 plan, the colonial church was organized as the first self-sufficient branch of the Dutch Reformed communion.

This new structure, arrived at after so much struggle, was not to last long. The Boston Tea Party was sending out its invitations. The beginning of revolutionary troubles in 1773 forced a break in correspondence with the mother church that would last till 1784.[11] By the time the American Revolution was over, the political context had completely changed. This was serious business for the two established churches, the Anglican and the Dutch Reformed. All of their colonial privileges had ended, and the Dutch Reformed church was not used to seeing itself as a "free church." The far-sighted Livingston saw the implications of this in 1783, before the revolutionary dust had settled, as is evident in a letter he wrote to his brother-in-law, the venerable Dominé Eilardus Westerlo of Albany:

> The revolution in our political interests has made a change in the general face of our American world, and as it has removed some difficulties which were taken into consideration in our former plan, so it has introduced

others which deserve a very weighty and impartial discussion.[12]

This "very weighty and impartial discussion" occupied the Dutch church over the next decade.[13]

The new United States was a great experiment: How shall a European-style but independent nation exist in a New World, set free from the hold of Europe's ancient laws and patterns? The final quarter of the eighteenth century was a time of constitution making in general.[14] The various American colonies were recasting their colonial charters as written constitutions. In 1777, the Continental Congress had already constituted a national government with the Articles of Confederation, but that frame of government was proving to be unsatisfactory, and so the American states began their own "very weighty and impartial discussion" at the Annapolis Convention of 1786.[15] At the subsequent Philadelphia Convention of 1787, a new Federal Constitution was drafted. In 1788 it was ratified, and by 1789 all the states were in.[16]

The parallel process in the Dutch church started earlier and took a little longer. The 1771 Plan of Union began to be modified at the 1785 meeting of the General Assembly, when the church declared itself to be a "synod" with several "classes."[17] The adoption of these names had the effect of claiming the same status for the North American Synod as any one of the provincial synods of the Netherlands, of quietly repudiating the appellate power of Classis Amsterdam, and of elevating the daughter church to the status of sisterhood.

In the meantime, the language problem demanded attention. The cultural changes which led to the Revolution only accelerated after it. The fifteen years following the Revolution saw the Dutch church switch from an almost total use of the Dutch language to an almost total use of English.[18] Why so fast, after 150 years of stoutly maintaining Dutch worship under British rule? The first reason is that members of the Dutch church had ceased to be British subjects. No longer must they be reluctant participants in the English culture. Now both English and Dutch were equal as Americans. The second reason is that, with the new freedom from England and the Anglican establishment, all churches were equal, and all had the right to incorporate and to own property. The Dutch language was no longer required to preserve the Reformed church's special status and its royal charters.

Before the Revolution, there was only one congregation that had regular English services, the church in "New-York City." Dominé Archibald Laidlie began his English preaching in 1763, and four years later the New-York consistory published an English language service book for its own use. The book included a full metrical Psalter in the Dutch style as well as translations of the Heidelberg Catechism, the Belgic Confession, and the Netherlands Liturgy. Within a couple of years after the Revolution, fully half of the congregations were scheduling English services, and there was need for a new service book. When the General Assembly began to meet again, it immediately took up the project. By 1789 the *Psalms and Hymns of the Reformed Dutch Church* was published, which included the New-York translations of the Catechism, Confession, and Liturgy, but which had a new Psalter to replace New-York's.

In a way, the book of *Psalms and Hymns* was constitutional because it was the sufficient means by which Dutch Reformed congregations were founded and believers built up in their faith. If one had the psalmbook and the Bible, one had everything needful to be formed as a good Dutch Reformed church member. But the leaders of the church recognized that a full-fledged and formal church constitution required not only the basic items of religious formation, but also the rules by which the church governed itself at every level, the rules by which it defined itself over against the civil government, and the dogmas by which it defined itself over against other brands of Christianity. And this too would have to be published in English.

Toward this end, the "very weighty and impartial discussion" was taken up by the synod of 1788, as recorded in its minutes:

> CHURCH ORDER: Since the circumstances of our church, especially in relation to the general protection of the civil authorities in freedom of worship, necessarily demand that not only the Confession of Faith, but also the Order of our Church and its Form of Government, should be made known to our countrymen in the English

language by the press, as has already been done by all the chief persuasions in our American States; and since the English language is our national tongue, and is making progress, and has already been adopted wholly or in part in worship in the most of our congregations, and the rising generation seem to be little acquainted with the Dutch tongue: the Synod therefore feel themselves bound, both as regards our fellow-citizens and the civil government in general, and also for the preservation of our Dutch Church and the instruction of its adherents, and of the children in particular to attend to this subject. Whereupon, it is resolved to appoint a committee to translate into the English language the Articles of Church Government of the National Synod, held at Dordrecht, 1618 and 1619, which, being accompanied by such articles taken from the proceedings of this Rev. Body as have particular reference to the circumstances of the Church in this country, will exhibit the true nature and form of government of our Dutch churches in America.[19]

These minutes indicate that the synod realized that its situation was different from that of the nation. The thirteen colonies had had to come up with something totally new. But the Dutch churches in America already had something they called the "Netherlandish Constitution." The problem was that this constitution was actually a section of the laws of the Dutch Province of North Holland. They set out to "bring their constitution home" from Europe, just as the nation of Canada would do two centuries later. The synod appointed a committee which included the best scholars in the denomination, Livingston, Westerlo, Jacobus Hardenbergh, Hermanus Meyer, and Dirck Romeyn.[20]

The committee had not finished its work in time for the Synod of 1789,[21] but in 1790 it was able to report as follows:

CHURCH ORDER. The report of the Rev. Committee upon this subject was presented:

1. That the distinct translations of the articles of Church Order of the Rev. Synod of Dordrecht in the years 1618 and 1619, and of the Plan of Union adopted 1772, both

made in English by Ds. Dirck Romeyn and Eil. Westerlo, be referred to a committee, who shall carefully compare the same with the original Dutch, and alter and amend all such English words and phrases as either are not pure, or do not actually and appropriately express the true and literal meaning.

2. That the same committee likewise prepare some observations upon the articles of Church Order, to be incorporated among them, in which the proper sense and meaning of them, if necessary, shall be briefly declared, or sufficient reasons be assigned why some articles are not inserted, or cannot be carried out in our American churches.

3. That the Rev. Ministers of the congregation of New York, as residing in close proximity to each other, and most conveniently situated readily to confer together, be appointed a committee on the subject by this Synod.

4. That in the coming spring, an extra Synod be convoked in order to revise said Plan of Union, and with common consent enlarge it, by inserting or adding some further rules, made in subsequent Convenings or Synods, and thus, upon previous investigation, approving *Synodaliter* the foresaid translation and observations.

5. That if necessary, the following autumn, a General Ecclesiastical Meeting be solicited, calmly to weigh the whole subject, and determine *formaliter*, whether the same shall be issued in full or in part, and in what language, or whether both in Dutch and English, for the special benefit of our congregations.[22]

This report, especially articles 2 and 4, shows that the original project of translating the Church Order and the Plan of Union had expanded. The committee was now to consider the revision of both documents, if necessary, and the addition of some "observatory" articles which would explain how, in the new American context, to fulfill the old Church Order. The committee had also to prepare the denomination for a more basic rethinking of its constitution.

At a special session of the synod in May, 1791, the committee was able to report its own rethinking:

> CHURCH ORDER. The gentlemen appointed a
> committee to specify the subjects to be included in the
> Constitution of the Reformed Dutch churches of America,
> to be issued in accordance with the intentions of Synod,
> report, that after mature deliberation, it appears to them
> that such publication should be entirely restricted to what
> constitutes the Doctrine, Liturgy, and Government of said
> churches, that it may not only not form an unnecessarily
> large volume, but also not perplex the English reader, by
> the introduction of anything that does not essentially
> pertain to our ecclesiastical regulations;...[23]

This recommendation was intended to keep the new document as
short and functional as possible. But for another reason this
recommendation was pivotal to the future of the denomination. It
was the first official use of the threefold phrase, "Doctrine,
Liturgy, and Government," to define the constitution of the
Reformed church. The phrase is still in use today.[24] This
definition meant that the constitution of the church would not be
limited to the rules of Government in the Church Order. The
formal constitution of the church was seen to be something larger
than a narrowly legal constitution. In fact, all of the Dutch canon
law of the typical *Kerkelyk Hantboekjes* would be replaced by
Doctrine and Liturgy. It also meant that the church could change
neither its Confession (the Doctrinal Standards) nor its Liturgy
without changing itself.

The committee's report to the synod of 1791 also suggested that
the Church Order and the Plan of Union be completely recast as a
new Church Order adapted to North America. In this way all the
charters and standing corporations could be preserved under the
new laws of the land. The relationship to the church in the
Netherlands would be defined and maintained.[25] The
recommendations of the committee were wholly accepted by the
synod. The committee was requested "to frame a draft of Church
Government and Discipline, agreeably to the principles stated in
the report," and have it ready for the next regular synod, in
October, 1791. Because of the importance of a brand new Church

Order, it was decided to hold the coming session in the style of convention, every congregation being invited to send delegates.[26]

At the October convention, the committee was ready with its draft, prepared by Dominé Livingston. It was read to the synod, and revised "article by article." The synod did not want to rush things, apparently. Another committee was appointed to revise the whole thing again and to report to a special session of the synod in the Spring of 1792.[27]

When the Extraordinary Synod met in May, 1792, the report of the committee suggested a change in plans back to a more conservative approach. The Church Order of Dort would be maintained after all, but it would be accompanied by some "explanatory articles:"

> CHURCH ORDER. Professor Livingston reports, in the name of the committee, that upon mature consideration of this subject, it appears to them that, besides a translation of the articles Syn. Dord., it will be necessary to add some articles in explanation of the way and manner in which said Church Order of Dord. is put into practice, agreeably to the Articles of Union ordained 1771, to the end that thus from one or the other the people in general may be able to form a correct conception of our mode of Church Government. He further informed the Rev. Body, that not only was the translation of said articles *Syn. Nationis* completed, but in part, also, the draft of the explanatory articles; and *Deo volente*, they would be ready to be presented for approval at the next Synod in October. *Resolved*, That the Rev. Body in the highest manner approve of such mode of exhibiting their form of Church Government, and will expect that all the papers pertaining thereto will be carefully presented at the Synod which is to be held at New York the coming October.[28]

This proposal was the first use of the term "Explanatory Articles." These were to be appended to the Church Order, with full legal weight (in much the same way that the "Bill of Rights" was added to the U.S. Constitution). The plan was approved.

The final draft of the Explanatory Articles was presented to the

October, 1792, meeting of the synod, and it was adopted. The whole set of materials was ordered to be published. The care of it was given to Livingston, with his colleague in New York, William Linn, and Elder Peter Wilson, from the same congregation.[29] The book was printed in 1793 by William Durell of New York City, under the title, *The Constitution of the Reformed Dutch Church, in the United States of America.* As planned, the book contained the Church's Doctrine, Liturgy, and Government. The contents were arranged as follows:

> Confession of Faith.
> Heidelberg Catechism.
> Compendium of the Christian Religion.
> Liturgy.
> Canons.
> Rules of Church Government, &c.
> Articles explanatory of Government and Discipline.

The Rules of Church Government were the Church Order of Dort. The Compendium was a translation of the *Kort Begrip*, a children's version of the catechism, which ordinarily accompanied it.

The book also included an important preface, which was probably written by Livingston.[30] The preface is characterized by a confessional tone. It states that by means of the book the Reformed church "presents her Constitution to the public" no less than for her own use, and this was precisely the original motivation for getting the whole project started, as mentioned in the quotation from the synod of 1788, above. The preface outlines the threefold shape of the constitution. It also points out that the familiar traditions of established church government will no longer be possible in the free church atmosphere of America, and that this is a good thing. On the whole, the preface is a wonderful and instructive little essay, and deserves to be kept available to the Reformed church. It is included in full in chapter five.

The published *Constitution* was presented to the synod of 1793. The synod recognized that the labor of its self-definition had come to an end after a decade of patient effort. It resolved the following:

CHURCH ORDER. The issuing of the Constitution of the Reformed Dutch churches in America having been regarded as a matter of great importance, and measures having been taken by many successive Synods to carry the same into execution; and the proposal of Professor Livingston, made in the Extra Synod of May, 1792, to embrace, in certain explanatory articles, a general account of the government and discipline of the Dutch churches, as well as the particular manner in which the regulations adopted in the last National Synod, held in Dordrecht, are to be followed, and applied to local circumstances in America, having been likewise received, and said explanatory articles placed upon the table of the General Synod, held in New York, in October, 1792; the translation also of the Ecclesiastical Rules of said Synod of Dordrecht having been unanimously approved, and orders given that the whole should be committed to the press: Professor Livingston, in the name of the committee, reported to this Body, that the same had been happily completed, and exhibited the book containing the Liturgy and Government of the Church, embraced in the Ecclesiastical Rules, and Explanatory Articles of the Reformed Dutch Churches in America. Agreeably to the foregoing resolutions of the Synod, Synod received the same with full approbation, and with thanksgivings to the Lord Jesus Christ, on whose shoulders is the government of the Church, and who has hitherto preserved and blessed the Reformed Church, and enabled its members to present their Constitution in a manner which they regard acceptable to Him; and not without expectation that the same will be contemplated with satisfaction by other persuasions, being convinced that it will subserve the promotion of piety and good order in the respective congregations. The Rev. Synod, therefore, with all earnestness, recommend this publication to all their congregations, and cannot, at the same time, refrain from testifying their thankfulness to the members of the committee appointed to carry forward this work. [31]

Undoubtedly the synod was not only thankful but relieved that the work was done, and that the "very weighty and impartial discussion" had borne fruit.

When the above resolution states the synod was "not without expectation that the same will be contemplated with satisfaction by other persuasions," it reveals that the larger church understood the confessional character of the *Constitution* as the preface had described it. Whether "other persuasions" actually took notice of the *Constitution* is difficult to determine. But it is clear that the Dutch Reformed Church in North America had taken an important evolutionary step ahead of the church in the Netherlands. While the latter continued to be a "reformed national church," the North American denomination had become a "confessional church," free from political sponsorship.[32] To adapt the full Calvinist ecclesiology of the "Netherlandish Constitution" to the American free church environment was an untried and risky experiment. But there was no other choice.

In 1793 the printed *Constitution* was officially received by "the Reverend Synod of Reformed Dutch Churches in North America."[33] This was the last synod on the provincial level to be the highest assembly of the North American church. Hereafter, in accordance with the Church Order of Dort, there would be a triennial General Synod as well as the annual Particular Synod. The 1794 General Synod was the first such synod on the national level to meet since the Synod of Dort itself in 1619.[34] As of 1794, therefore, the Reformed Dutch Church in North America was wholly based and operating on its own constitution.

The synod of 1793 was also the last one to use the Dutch language. The General Synod of 1794 decided to record its meetings in both Dutch and English and to consider the English minutes "as original and authentic."[35] It had been only thirty years since the first English preacher had been brought to New York. In that span of time, the denomination had become wholly a North American church, in which even a highly ranking churchman from the Netherlands could now have but little to say. The door had now been opened to being a non-ethnic church. In principle, at least, membership had more to do with shared convictions than with shared ancestry.

The distinctive three-fold shape of the constitution of the

Reformed church has been maintained to this day, although much within it has been revised over the years. The story of its history since 1793 is told in chapter six. But from 1793 on, the distinctive three-fold constitution has continued to differentiate the Reformed church from the other Calvinistic bodies in North America. What is remarkable about the three-fold shape is that, unlike all the other Calvinistic bodies, the Dutch Reformed church assumed that its Liturgy was not an option. By including it in its constitution, the church recognized that the actual liturgical text was something that helped form the basic character of the church. Without it, the church would be essentially different. By contrast, the Congregational churches avoided liturgy altogether. The Presbyterian churches had no liturgy, and defined the worship of the church either by the rubrics of a Directory or the regulations of a Church Order. The Christian Reformed church has had a Liturgy, but it has governed worship by means of its Church Order, which requirs only that the synodically approved forms in the Liturgy be used, and these could be changed by any synod at will. But in the Reformed church, worship has been made only secondarily a matter of Church Order. The primary definition of worship comes from the actual text of the Liturgy itself, and from its use as a living document.

There is a lesson in the history contained in this chapter. When the representatives of the Dutch Reformed congregations began to gather in those first synodical meetings of the 1780s it was a time of crisis for the Reformed churches. Their mother tongue was in decline. They were still nursing the wounds of a serious schism. They were short on pastors. Some of the largest congregations had lost their established financial support. Their college, Queen's, in New Brunswick, was struggling to survive. The two states of New York and New Jersey had been particularly ravaged by the Revolution. There were many good arguments against trying to maintain their particular brand of Christianity in English-speaking North America. Already before the Revolution, no less than the Classis of Amsterdam had suggested that their North American congregations enter into an organic merger with the other Calvinistic bodies, especially the German Reformed and the Presbyterian.

But in the conviction that they had something that was worth maintaining, the early synods worked to find ways to keep their old church going in a new and unfamiliar world. The specific form that this work took was tending to their constitution, not from a motive of narrow self-absorption, but as part of their witness to the wider world. The Netherlandish Constitution had given them a good start, but since the cocoon of European law had fallen away, they would have to fly on wings of their own making. They had to consider what made them what they were, what was distinctive about them, and what they had in common with other churches. They had to determine what parts of their Dutch heritage they could do without and what parts had to be maintained or translated or adapted to the new situation. They had to determine which things were essential, which things could not be changed without actually changing themselves. They were asking, "What is the glue that holds us together?" They answered their questions with the constitution, translated, adapted, and updated; the three strong legs of Doctrine, Liturgy, and Government. On these three legs, and with renewed self-confidence, the Reformed church entered a new century of vigor, prosperity, steady expansion, and a profound sense of mission.

V

The Constitution:
Text and Commentary

The Constitution of the Reformed Church first appeared in 1793. Here follows a reproduction of that publication, with commentary interwoven. The full texts of the Preface, the Rules (Church Order) of Dort (1619), and the Articles Explanatory (1792) are included. In the 1793 edition, both the Rules of Dort and the Explanatory Articles are enumerated as "Articles," so in order to distinguish them, the commentary always refers to any of the Rules of Dort by the term "Rule" and restricts the term "Article" to the Explanatory Articles. The full texts of the (Belgic) Confession of Faith, the Heidelbergh Catechism, the Compendium, and the Liturgy are available elsewhere, so these have been included by title only. [1] The title page gives the name of the denomination as "The Reformed Dutch Church, in the United States of America." In 1793 the denomination had not yet settled on its proper name. The synodical psalmbooks of 1789 and 1796 used the more common style, "The Reformed Dutch Church in North America," which was the generally accepted name for several generations, with the adjective "Protestant" often inserted before "Dutch." In each of the rules of Dort, the key phrase was printed in italics, and this has been maintained.

THE

CONSTITUTION

OF THE

REFORMED DUTCH CHURCH,

IN THE

UNITED STATES

OF

AMERICA.

NEW - YORK:

Printed and Sold by WILLIAM DURELL, *at his Book-store and Printing Office, No. 19, Queen-Street, 1793.*

——

[WITH THE PRIVILEGE OF COPY RIGHT.]

PREFACE.

In consequence of that liberty wherewith Christ hath made his people free, it becomes their duty as well as privilege, openly to confess and worship him according to the dictates of their own consciences. To perform this aright, and bear a proper testimony against the heresies and false opinions which have always disturbed the peace and corrupted the purity of the Church, it has been found necessary to explain with candour and boldness, the articles of faith and discipline, and accurately to distinguish between truth and error. Whereever[2] such explanations constitute a bond of union wholly voluntary, and unattended with civil emoluments or penalties, they cannot be considered as an infringement upon the equal liberties of others, or as fixing boundaries and terms of communion, inimical to Christian Charity. The unerring word of God remaining the only standard of the Faith and Worship of his people, they can never incur the charge of presumption, in openly declaring, what to them appears to be the mind and will of their divine Lord and Master.

The Church is a Society, wholly distinct in its principles, laws and end, from any which men have ever instituted for civil purposes. It consists of all, in every age and place, who are chosen, effectually called, and united by faith to the Lord Jesus Christ. The different dispensations, either before, or since the coming of the Messiah, have made no essential change in the benefits of the everlasting Covenant; nor do the various denominations, or discriptions[2] of particular Churches, under which, from many unavoidable circumstances of language, nation, or other causes of distinction, believers are classed, effect any schism in the body, or destroy the communion of saints.

At the reformation it was judged proper by all the Churches to ratify and publish their respective creeds and the adopted forms of their ecclesiastical governments. In America, since the late happy revolution, the Churches of different denominations have found it necessary to organize themselves, agreeably to the present state in which the good providence of God hath placed them, and have already published their several constitutions. The reformed Dutch Church has been prevented by some particular circumstances from accomplishing this desirable and important object, at an earlier period. She has now completed the translations which were necessary, and presents her constitution to the public.

To the Constitution of a Church appertains its **DOCTRINES,** *mode of* **WORSHIP,** *and* **GOVERNMENT.** *When these are known, its true and distinguishing character is sufficiently ascertained.*

The **DOCTRINES** *of the reformed Dutch Church are comprised in the Articles of Faith, the Catechism and Compendium, and in her Canons.*

Her mode of **WORSHIP** *is expressed in the Liturgy, where forms of several prayers are given, without any idea, however, of restraining her members to any particular terms or fixed standards for prayer. Firmly believing, that the gifts of the Holy Spirit for the edification of Zion in every age, are promised and bestowed, the reformed Dutch Church judges it sufficient to shew in a few specimens the general tenor and manner in which public worship is performed, and leaves it to the piety and gifts of her ministers to conduct the ordinary solemnities of the sanctuary, in a manner they judge most acceptable to God, and most edifying to his people.*

Her **GOVERNMENT** *and discipline are contained in the rules of Church Government, ratified in the last National Synod held at Dordrecht: these are illustrated in the Explanatory Articles, and applied to the circumstances and local situation of the Church. As many of the articles in the rules are sufficiently plain and applicable without any elucidation, such only are mentioned in the Explanatory Articles which were judged most* *necessary to give a connected and just view of the government of the Church as now established in America.*

An expression which occurs in the 18th. and 36th. Articles of faith, and which mentions the Anabaptists in harsh terms, will probably with some, especially such as are ignorant of the history of the sixteenth century, appear unfriendly; and if applied to those who are sometimes distinguished at this day by the same name, be considered as an assertion not founded in truth. To obviate every objection it will suffice to observe, that there were persons at, and shortly after the reformation who were called by that name, who held the erroneous and seditious sentiments which in those articles are rejected, and who by their fanaticism and extravagance rendered themselves abhorred by all sober and religious men. In publishing the articles of faith, the Church determined to abide by the words adopted in the Synod of Dordrecht, as most expressive of what she believes to be truth; in consequence of which, the terms alluded to, could not be avoided. But she openly and candidly declares, that she by no means thereby intended to refer to any denomination of Christians at present known, and would be grieved at giving offence, or unnecessarily hurting the feelings of any person.

Whatever relates to the immediate authority and interposition of the magistrates in the government of the Church, and which is introduced more or less, into all the national establishments in Europe, is intirely[2] omitted in the constitution now published. Whether the Church of Christ will not be more effectually patronized in a civil government where full freedom of conscience and worship is equally protected and insured to all men, and where truth is left to vindicate her own sovereign authority and influence, than where men in power promote their favorite denominations by temporal emoluments and partial discriminations, will now, in America, have a fair trial; and all who know and love the truth will rejoice in the prospect which such a happy situation affords for the triumph of the gospel, and the reign of peace and love.

COMMENTARY on the Preface:

We are not certain who wrote the preface. There are at least two indications, though, which point to John Henry Livingston. First, the opening words of the preface are remarkably similar to the opening of the preface to the 1789 Episcopal Prayer Book.[3] We know that Livingston had his eye on the Episcopal church, his having borrowed from the Anglican Psalter to produce the 1789 *Psalms and Hymns* for the synod. Second, the reference in the preface to "the everlasting Covenant" is characteristic Livingston language.[4] In any case, we do know that Livingston was the editor responsible for the *Constitution* going to press, so he is the most likely author of the preface.

The first paragraph is an apology for the whole book. Its message is that the Reformed church, by publishing its *Constitution*, does not thereby "infringe upon the equal liberties" of other denominations which differ in doctrine and practice. (This is certainly a wholly different attitude than that of the 1619 Synod of Dort with which the Reformed church was claiming continuity.) The paragraph also establishes the Reformed church as a *confessional* church, with its members having the "duty as well as privilege, openly to confess and worship [Christ] according to the dictates of their own consciences," and that, "to perform this aright, and bear a proper testimony...it has been found necessary to explain with candour and boldness, the Articles of Faith and Discipline." In other words, the church is known and defined by its testimony and confession. That means that the book has not only an internal value for the church which has produced it, but also an external value for the larger world. Within the new free church environment of the United States, the Reformed Dutch Constitution must "openly declare what appears to them" to be the truth, and this cannot be judged "presumptuous."

The second paragraph is remarkable. It begins in orthodox Reformed fashion by defining the church according to the Heidelberg Catechism ("all, in every age and place, who are chosen" and "united by faith to the Lord Jesus Christ," Answer 54) and the Canons of Dort ("effectually called," Chapter I, Article

7). But it then argues for the essential transdenominational unity of the church on these grounds: since in scripture, the "different dispensations" of the covenants did not detract from the essential unity of the "Everlasting Covenant," so the fact that the church is divided as a result of "many unavoidable circumstances" does not effect any division or schism in the communion of saints. In other words, the Reformed church is one among many denominations, which, in spite of their differences in custom, usages, and government, are essentially one body.

This essential unity does not remove the rationale for a particular church to maintain its distinctive identity, so long as it explains why. Appealing to the Reformation, when "all the Churches ratified and published their respective creeds and the adopted forms of their ecclesiastical governments," the Reformed church finds precedence to publish its own. (Indeed, other denominations already had.) Thus, the book has a *confessional* purpose, and its appearance was necessary, not only for home use, but also so that the Reformed church might "present her constitution to the public."

The preface goes on to outline the threefold shape of the *Constitution*: Doctrines, Worship, and Government. The Doctrines "are comprised in the Articles of Faith [i.e. the Belgic Confession], the [Heidelberg] Catechism and Compendium [by Faukelius], and in her Canons [of Dort.]" The preface fails to report that the text of the canons was greatly reduced by the deletion of the "Rejection of Errors" section in each of the four chapters. Although this may have been done in order to soften the perceived stringent tone of the canons, it had the effect of removing some of the document's best biblical exposition.

The next paragraph says that the church's "mode of Worship is expressed in the Liturgy." The Reformed Dutch church has been unique among Calvinist bodies in maintaining a full-fledged Liturgy. But the precise status of the Liturgy is qualified by the statement, "The forms of several prayers are given without any idea, however, of restraining her members to any particular terms or fixed standards for prayer." The preface steps away from the received Dutch discipline by suggesting a voluntary use of the Liturgy, or at least some parts of it. The Synod of Dort had made the strict use of the Liturgy obligatory, including the particular prayers within it. This rule continued in force throughout the next two centuries in the Netherlands.[5] The Liturgy had sometimes to be enforced on unwilling pastors, especially those who espoused the Puritan and Presbyterian view that prayer should be totally free, a view that later came to be held by the pietists.[6] The preface obviously argues for the "free prayer" view. Perhaps this attitude only reflects the prevailing practice of the time, but it signals that, officially, at least, a step had been taken: the Liturgy will remain constitutional, but its use will be minimally enforced. Only those parts will be mandatory which are specifically mentioned in the relevant rules of the Church Order, such as the Forms for Baptism, Holy Communion, Ordinations, and Excommunication.

The paragraph on Government and Discipline briefly introduces the Rules of Dort and the Explanatory Articles. The paragraph after that apologizes for the strong language against the Anabaptists in two articles of the Belgic Confession. It is a little dishonest, perhaps, for the preface to state that the articles do not "refer to any denomination of Christians at present known."[7] The Reformed Dutch must hold to their historic confession, but they don't want to hurt anyone's feelings!

The final paragraph points to the most crucial matter of all: the fact of total disestablishment. The "Netherlandic Constitution" had simply assumed that the Reformed church was an established church and well deserving of the "temporal emoluments and partial discriminations" of "men in power." But the First Amendment to the U.S. Constitution, published only three years before the preface, stated that "Congress shall make no law respecting an establishment of religion, or prohibiting the free exercise thereof." It was only natural, then, that most of the material relating to the ecclesiastical interests of the magistrate should be omitted from the Rules of Dort,[8] with the necessary adjustments made in the Explanatory Articles.

Then, making virtue out of necessity, the preface faces the "free exercise" of religion. All the denominations would now be living under "a civil government where full freedom of conscience is equally protected and insured to all men." It is an auspicious moment in history. "Whether the Church of Christ will not be more effectually patronised" where all churches are free, and where "truth is left to vindicate her own sovereign authority and influence...will now, in America, have a fair trial." The preface has arrived at a single solution to the two weightiest problems facing the Reformed Dutch church—its relation to the state and its relation to other denominations. And in language that is optimistic and generous, the preface ends on the same confessional note on which it began, "All who know and love the truth will rejoice in the prospect which such a happy situation affords for the triumph of the Gospel, and the reign of peace and love."

CONTENTS

CONFESSION OF FAITH

ART.

I. One only GOD.

II. By what means GOD is made known unto us.

III. Of the written word of GOD.

IV. Canonical books of the Holy Scripture.

V. From whence the Holy Scriptures derive their dignity and authority.

VI. The difference between the canonical and apocryphal books.

VII. The sufficiency of the Holy Scriptures to be the only rule of faith.

VIII. That GOD is one, in essence, yet nevertheless distinguished in three persons.

IX. The proof of the Trinity of persons.

X. Jesus Christ is true and eternal GOD.

XI. The Holy Ghost is true and eternal GOD.

XII. Of the Creation.

XIII. Of Divine Providence.

XIV. Creation and Fall of Man, and his incapacity to perform what is truly good.

XV. Original Sin.

XVI. Election eternal.

XVII. Man's Recovery.

XVIII. Incarnation of Jesus Christ.

XIX. Union and distinction of the two natures in the person of Christ.

XX. God hath manifested his righteousness and mercy in Christ.

XXI. Satisfaction of Christ, our only High-Priest, for us.

XXII. Justification through faith in Christ.

XXIII. Our Justification consists in the forgiveness of sin, and the imputation of Christ's obedience.

XXIV. Sanctification and good Works.

XXV. The ceremonial Law abolished.

XXVI. Christ's Intercession.

XXVII. The Catholic Christian Church.

XXVIII. Every one is bound to join the true Church.

XXIX. Marks of the true Church, and wherein she differs from the false Church.

XXX. Government and Offices in the Church.

XXXI. Of Ministers, Elders, and Deacons.

XXXII. Order and Discipline of the Church.

XXXIII. Of Sacraments.

XXXIV. Baptism.

XXXV. The Lord's Supper.

XXXVI. Of Magistrates.

XXXVII. Of the last Judgment.

Heidelbergh Catechism.

Compendium of the Christian Religion.

LITURGY.

Of public Prayer.
Administration of Baptism.
Administration of the Lord's Supper.
Form of Excommunication.
Form of readmitting excommunicated Persons.
Form for ordaining Ministers.
Form for ordaining Elders and Deacons.
Confirmation of Marriage.
The Consolation of the Sick.
The Confession of Faith, composed in the Council of Nice, in the
    year 325.
The Creed of Athanasius, written in the year 333.

CANONS.

Of Divine Predestination.
Of the Death of Christ, and Redemption thereby.
Man's Corruption, his Conversion to God, and the manner
thereof.
Perseverance of the Saints.
Conclusion of the Canons.

Rules of Church Government, &c.

Chap.
I. Of the Offices.
II. Ecclesiastical Assemblies.
III. Doctrine, Sacraments, and Usages.
IV. Christian Discipline.

Articles explanatory of Government and Discipline.

Ministers of the Word.
Professors of Theology.
Elders and Deacons.
Ecclesiastical Assemblies.
Consistories.
Form of a Call.
Classes.
Particular Synods.
General Synod.
Usages and Customs.
Of Discipline.

THE CONFESSION OF FAITH OF THE *REFORMED CHURCHES*, In the NETHERLANDS.

Revised in the NATIONAL SYNOD, last held at DORTRECHT, in the Years 1618 and 1619.

THE
HEIDELBERGH CATECHISM.

A
COMPENDIUM
OF THE
CHRISTIAN RELIGION
For those who intend to approach
THE HOLY SUPPER OF THE LORD.

THE
LITURGY
OF THE REFORMED CHURCH IN
NETHERLAND.
Or, the Forms used therein in Public
Worship.

I. Of Public Prayer.
II. Of the Administration of the Holy Sacraments.
III. Of the Exercise of Church Discipline.
IV. Of the Ordination of Church Officers.
V. Of the celebration of Marriage.
VI. Of Comforting the Sick.

Christian Prayers, to be used in the assembly of the Faithful, and on other occasions.

A Prayer on the Lord's day, before sermon.
A Prayer to be used on the Lord's Day, after Sermon.
A Prayer before the explanation of the Catechism.
A Prayer after the explanation of the Catechism.
A Prayer before sermon in the week.
A Prayer after sermon in the week.
A Morning Prayer.
An evening Prayer.
A Prayer at the opening of the consistory.
A Prayer at the close of the Consistory.
A Prayer at the meeting of the Deacons.
Grace before Meat.
Grace after Meat.
A Prayer for sick and tempted Persons.
The form for the Administration of
Baptism, to Infants of Believers.
The form for the Administration of holy
baptism, to adult persons.
The Form for the Administration of the
LORD's SUPPER.
The FORM of EXCOMMUNICATION.
The form of re-admitting excommunicated
persons into the church of Christ.
Form for Ordaining the Ministers of
God's Word.
The Form for ordaining Elders and Dea-
cons, when ordained at the same time.
The Form for the Confirmation of
Marriage, before the Church.
The consolation of the sick, which is an
instruction in faith, and the way of salva-
tion to prepare believers to die willingly.

The Confession of Faith, composed in the Council of Nice, in the year of our Lord, 325. The Creed of Saint Athanasius, Bishop of Alexandria, written in the year of our Lord, 333.

CANONS

Ratified in the National Synod of the reformed Church, held at *Dordrecht*, in the Years, 1618 and 1619.

FIRST HEAD OF DOCTRINE.

Of DIVINE PREDESTINATION.

SECOND HEAD OF DOCTRINE.

Of the Death of Christ, and the redemption of Men thereby.

THE THIRD AND FOURTH HEADS OF DOCTRINE

Of the Corruption of Man, his Conversion to God, and the Manner thereof.

THE FIFTH HEAD OF DOCTRINE.

Of the Perseverance of the Saints.

R U L E S

OF

CHURCH

GOVERNMENT

ESTABLISHED

IN THE

NATIONAL

SYNOD,

HELD IN

DORDRECHT,

IN THE YEARS

1618 AND 1619.

ART. I.

For the maintenance of good order in the church of Christ, it is necessary there should be certain *Offices* and *Assemblies*, and a strict attention to *Doctrines, Sacraments,* and *Usages*, and *Christian Discipline*, of all which the following ecclesiastical ordinances particularly treat:

I. OF THE OFFICES

ART. II.

The *Offices* in the church of Christ are fourfold, viz.
1. The office of *Ministers of the Word.*
2. The office of *Teachers of Theology.*
3. The office of *Elders.*
4. The office of *Deacons.*

The original Dutch version, in Rule 1, has "Ceremonies" instead of "Usages," and in Rule 2, has "Doctors" instead of "Teachers of Theology." The word "Doctor" had a more general meaning at the time.

ART. III.

No person although he be a teacher of Theology, Elder or Deacon, shall be permitted to officiate in the ministry of the word, and sacraments, without being thereunto *lawfully called*; and whenever any one offends herein, and shall persist after repeated admonitions, the classis shall determine whether he shall be proceeded against as a schismatic, or punished in some other way.

The Dutch says: whenever any one "acts to the contrary" he shall be "declared a schismatic."

ART. IV.

A *lawful call* to persons heretofore not engaged in the ministry of the word, consists, 1st. *In a free choice* made by the consistory and deacons after previous fasting and prayer, and advising with the classis where it has been customary to apply to them for council. 2nd. *In an examination*, or enquiry into the doctrine and morals of the person so elected, which shall be performed by the classis, in the presence of the deputies of the synod, or some of them. 3d. *In the approbation* of the members in full communion with the church to which he is called; for the obtaining of which, the name of such minister shall be published in the church, three Sabbaths successively, that opportunity may be given for stating lawful objection if any there be. 4th. *In public ordination*, in the presence of the congregation, according to the form adopted for that purpose, accompanied with suitable engagements, exhortations, prayers, and imposition of hands by the minister who presides at the ordination, and such other ministers as may be present. Provided however that imposition of hands may be performed by the classical assembly in the case of persons ordained as missionaries to form congregations in distant settlements, or to serve in churches that are under persecution.

The "form adopted for that purpose" refers to the *Form for ordaining Ministers* of the Liturgy, which is also printed in the *Constitution*. The Dutch rule requires "proper correspondence with the Christian Magistrates of the particular place" no less than the "advice of the Classis," and after the examination by the classis, "the *Approbation* and assent of the Civil Authority, and subsequently also by the members of the Reformed Congregation in that place." This right of the magistrate had first entered the Church Order in 1578. The provision "to form congregations in distant settlements" is not in the Dutch. The changes testify to the disestablishment of the church and to its frontier missions.

ART. V.

With respect to those already engaged in the ministry, and who are *called to another congregation*, such call shall be made in manner before mentioned, by the consistory and deacons, with the advice or approbation of the classis; to which the minister so called shall produce good ecclesiastical credentials of his doctrine and morals, and shall after publication in the church for three Sabbaths successively, as above mentioned, be installed under previous engagements, accompanied with prayer.

In this rule, too, the Dutch version requires the "approval by the Magistrate of the particular place" before the name may be published in the congregation. The Dutch has the following at the end of this rule: "In short, in that which has been said before, if anyone has a clear right of presentation [patronage], or any other right, as much as it can be exercised efficaciously, without injury to God's Church and to good Church Order, may it please the Higher Authorities and the Synods of the respective Provinces to give attention to it, and for the good of the churches to put it to necessary order." *Patronage* was the right of certain nobles or civic officials to appoint pastors to specific positions. Those who had the right were reluctant to give it up, and since they usually had political power, the church was unsuccessful in its attempts to cancel their rights (Patronage caused even more trouble in Scotland.)

ART. VI.

No minister shall be at liberty to accept of the charge of any particular service as *chaplain*, unless he is previously admitted, and qualified according to the preceding articles; nor shall the acceptance of such service exempt him from being subject equally with others to the discipline of the church.

The Dutch specifically mentions chaplaincies in private manor houses and hospitals.

ART. VII.

No person shall be ordained to the ministry of the word without settling in some congregation, unless he be sent as a *missionary* to churches under persecution, or employed to gather congregations, where none have as yet been established.

ART. VIII.

Schoolmasters, mechanics, or others, who have not *regularly studied* shall not be admitted to the office of the ministry, unless the best assurance be obtained of their singular talents, piety, humility, sobriety, good understanding, and discretion, together with the gifts of utterance. Whenever therefore such persons offer themselves for the ministry, the classis having first obtained the approbation of the synod, shall previously examine them, and, according to their proficiency, shall enjoin a course of private exercises, after which they shall be dealt with as shall be judged most conducive to edification.

The Dutch has "artisans" instead of "mechanics."

ART. IX.

Noviciates, popish priests, and monks, together with those who *forsake other sects*, shall not be admitted to the service of the church without great care, and circumspection, nor until after a certain time of previous trial.

The word "noviciates" translates *nieuwelingen*, which really means "neophyte," in the sense of a new convert.

ART. X.

A minister being lawfully called may not *forsake the church, or congregation* where he is regularly settled in order to accept a call elsewhere without obtaining the previous consent of the consistory and deacons, and of those who have formerly borne those offices, together with the approbation of the classis. And in like manner shall no church be permitted to receive him, before he has produced sufficient credentials of his regular dismission from the church, and classis where he last officiated.

The Dutch requires the approval of the magistrate as well as the classis.

ART. XI.

In like manner the consistory as representing the congregation shall be bound to provide their Ministers with a *decent support,* and shall not forsake them without the knowledge, and decision of the classis, who also shall determine, on complaint made of a deficiency of support, whether such minister shall be removed, or not.

ART. XII.

A minister of the word being once lawfully called in manner before mentioned, is bound to the service of the sanctuary as long as he liveth. Therefore he shall not be at liberty to devote himself to a *secular vocation*, except for great and important reasons concerning which the classis, shall enquire and determine.

ART. XIII.

If a minister become *incapable* of performing the duties of his office, either through age, sickness, or otherwise, such minister shall, notwithstanding, retain the honour and stile of his office, and be provided with an honourable support by the churches to which he hath ministered; provision is in like manner to be made for the widows and orphans of ministers in general.

ART. XIV.

Whenever it shall become necessary that ministers, for the reasons before mentioned, or for any other cause, should *desist for a time* from the exercise of their office, (of which the

Consistory is the judge) they shall notwithstanding, continually be subject to the call of their congregations.

The Dutch text suggests a slightly weaker role for the consistory: "(which shall not happen without the advice of the Consistory)".

ART. XV.

No minister relinquishing the service of his own church, or being unattached to any particular congregation, shall be permitted to *preach indiscriminately* from place to place, without the consent and authority of the synod, or classis; in like manner no Minister may preach or administer the sacraments in any church other than his own, without the consent of the consistory of that church.

ART. XVI.

The *office of a MINISTER* is to persevere in prayer, and the ministry of the word, to dispense the sacraments, to watch over his brethren the Elders and Deacons, as well as over the whole congregation, and lastly in conjunction with the Elders, to exercise christian discipline and to be careful, that all things be done decently and in good order.

This rule reflects the description of the pastor's office that is within the liturgical *Form for ordaining Ministers.*

ART. XVII.

Among the ministers of the gospel *equality* shall be preserved in their ministerial labours, and as far as possible in other things, agreeably to such arrangements as the consistory, or if need be, the classis shall make. A similar equality shall also be maintained among the elders and deacons.

ART. XVIII.

The *office of the TEACHERS or PROFESSORS of Theology* is to explain the holy scriptures, and vindicate the pure doctrines of the gospel against heresy and error.

ART. XIX.

The congregations shall endeavour to raise public funds for the support of *students in theology.*

ART. XX.

In churches where a number of able ministers are settled, the practice of *discussing theological theses* shall be instituted, that by such exercises some may be prepared for the ministry; pursuing however therein, the special appointment and order of the general synod.

This would appear to be a continuation and modification of the late Reformation practice of "prophesying," when, monthly or even weekly, pastors would meet to discuss and interpret the scriptures in public.

ART. XXI.

The consistories in every congregation shall be careful to provide good *Schoolmasters,* who are able, not only to instruct children in reading, writing, grammar, and the liberal sciences; but also to teach them the catechism, and the first principles of religion.

"The liberal sciences" are "the liberal arts." This rule requires each consistory to sponsor a parochial school. Many of the early congregations which were able to did so. Soon after the

Revolution, most of these Reformed parochial schools were absorbed into the American common (public) school system, and that is what accounts for Explanatory Article LVI. At the initial stage of their absorption, when American culture was Protestant, the public schools were essentially non-denominational Christian schools, and, thus, still somewhat able to satisfy this rule. (Of course the public school has evolved into something else.) So the view is obviously a recent one that the Reformed church does not support Christian day-schools, as over against the Christian Reformed church, which does. On the other hand, this rule contradicts the Christian Reformed church's "Kuyperian" doctrine of "sphere sovereignty," which says that the Christian school should be independent of the institution of the church.

ART. XXII.

The *Elders shall be chosen* by the suffrages of the Consistory, and of the deacons: in making this choice it shall be lawful, as shall best suit the situation of each church, either to nominate as many elders, as shall be judged necessary, for the approbation of the members in full communion, and upon their being approved, and found acceptable, to confirm them with public prayers and engagements; or, to propose a double number, that the one half of those nominated may be chosen by the members, and in the same manner confirmed in their office. In either mode of election the confirmation is to be agreeable to the form, instituted for that purpose.

The Dutch version requires an election by the congregation only with the second alternative. The first alternative implies only that no objection be raised from the congregation upon successive announcement of the choices advanced by the consistory. The word *confirmation* translates the Dutch word *bevestigen*. The "form instituted for that purpose" is the *Form for ordaining Elders and Deacons* in the Liturgy. The Liturgy translates the word *bevestigen* as *ordination* (except in the *Form for Marriages*).

ART. XXIII.

The *office of ELDERS* (besides what is common to them with the ministers of the word, expressed in Art. XVI) is, to take heed that the ministers, together with their fellow elders and deacons, faithfully discharge their respective duties; and also, before, or after the Lord's Supper, as time and circumstances permit, and as shall be most for the edification of the congregation, to assist in performing visitations, in order particularly to instruct and comfort the members in full communion, as well as to exhort others to the regular profession of the christian religion.

This rule summarizes the description of the elder's office which is contained in the liturgical *Form for ordaining Elders and Deacons.* The ministers and the elders watch over each other mutually. The elders are also specifically called to visit and minister to the members of the congregation in connection with the Lord's Supper. This rule lies behind the excellent Dutch practice of *huisbezoek,* house-visitation, which is still practiced by many boards of elders in North America.

ART. XXIV.

The *Deacons shall be chosen*, approved, and confirmed in the same manner as the elders.

ART. XXV.

The *office peculiar to the DEACONS* is, diligently to collect the alms and other monies appropriated for the use of the poor, and with the advice of the consistory, cheerfully, and faithfully to distribute the same to strangers, as well as to those of their own household, according to the measure of their respective necessities; to visit, and comfort the distressed, and to be careful that the alms be not misused; of the distribution of which, they shall render an account in consistory at such time, as the said Consistory shall determine, and in the presence of so many of the congregation as may choose to attend.

This rule echoes the explanation of the deacon's office within the Liturgy's *Form for Ordaining Elders and Deacons*. The Dort Church Order assumes that the ministers' salaries and church building expenses be paid out of public funds collected and distributed by local government. Thus, the role of deacons here is simply that of ecclesiastical charity, following Acts 6. After the American Revolution, the government would no longer finance the church, and the role of the deacons would have to expand. See Explanatory Article XXVII.

ART. XXVI.

The deacons shall endeavour to maintain a good correspondence with the *overseers of Poor-houses*, and other public almoners, in order that the alms may be the better distributed among those, whose necessities are the greatest.

ART. XXVII.

The elders and deacons shall *serve two years,* and the one half be changed annually, and others appointed in their room, unless the situation or advantage of some particular churches should otherwise require.

ART. XXVIII.

As it is the duty of *christian Magistrates* to countenance the worship of God, to recommend religion by their example, and protect the members of the community in the full and regular exercise of religious liberty; so it is the duty of ministers, elders, and deacons, zealously and faithfully to inculcate upon all their congregations, that obedience, love, and homage, which they owe to the magistrates. All ecclesiastical persons shall, by their own good conduct, in this respect, give an example to the congregations, and, by becoming reverence, endeavour to excite, and maintain the favourable attention of government to the churches—to the end that each mutually fulfilling their respective duties in the fear of the Lord, all suspicion and jealousy may be prevented, and a happy confidence, conducive to the welfare of the churches, be preserved.

This rule reflects Article 36 of the Belgic Confession. What the Dutch actually says is that the magistrates are "to protect the Ministers, Elders, and Deacons, and to lend a hand to them in time of need." The change in the rule reflects American disestablishment, and that the government would no longer have a peculiar relationship with the institutional church, rather only with the individual citizens within the church.

II.

OF

ECCLESIASTICAL

ASSEMBLIES

ARTICLE XXIX.

The *ECCLESIASTICAL ASSEMBLIES*, which shall be maintained, are of four kinds, viz.

1. *Consistorial.*
2. *Classical.*
3. *The Particular Synod.*
4. *The General, or National Synod.*

ART. XXX.

In those assemblies, *ecclesiastical matters* only shall be transacted, and that in an ecclesiastical manner. A greater assembly shall take cognizance of those things alone which could not be determined in a lesser, or that appertain to the churches or congregations in general, which compose such an assembly.

ART. XXXI.

If any person conceive himself aggrieved by the decision of a lesser assembly, he shall have the liberty and right of *appealing* to a higher and that which is determined by a majority of voices in such assembly, shall be held decisive and binding, unless it can be demonstrated to be contrary to the word of God, and these articles.

ART. XXXII.

The *transactions* of all ecclesiastical assemblies shall begin with prayer, and conclude with thanksgiving.

The Dutch says, "shall begin with calling on God's name." Many archival minute-books use this idiom as a technical term. The Liturgy contains written prayers for use at the opening and closing of consistory, which were originally intended for all ecclesiastical assemblies.

ART. XXXIII.

Those who are delegated to attend the Assemblies shall bring with them *credentials,* and instructions, signed by those who send them, and such only shall be entitled to a decisive vote.

ART. XXXIV.

In all assemblies there shall be a president, and secretary. The business of the *Secretary* shall be to register whatever is deemed worthy of being entered on the minutes.

In both this rule and the following the Dutch has *Præses* for *President*. See Rule 41 below.

ART. XXXV.

The office of the *President* is to state and explain the business which is to be transacted—to preserve order—to silence the captious, and those who are too vehement in debate, and to inflict upon them proper censure in case of disobedience. The office of president shall cease when the assembly rises.

ART. XXXVI.

A Classis hath the same *jurisdiction* over a Consistory, which a particular Synod hath over a Classis, and a general Synod over a particular.

ART. XXXVII.

In all churches there shall be a *CONSISTORY* composed of the ministers and elders, who shall meet together at least once every week, and when met, the minister shall preside and moderate the business. If there be a plurality of ministers, they shall preside and direct in rotation.

The Dutch adds an important stipulation: "And the Magistracy of the place may, if it so desires, have at the Consistory one or two of its number, being members of the Congregation, to listen to, and join in deliberating on the matters that come up." This right of the magistrate first appears in the Hague Church Order of 1586.

ART. XXXVIII.

No *new Consistory* shall be constituted in any particular place without the previous advice, and concurrence of the classis; and where the number of elders is too small, the deacons may be admitted as members of the Consistory.

The admittance of deacons to the consistory was always a rarity in the Netherlands, but it became the usual practice in North America because of the small size of most of the congregations.

ART. XXXIX.

In places where a *Consistory hath not yet been formed,* the duties otherwise imposed by this constitution upon the consistory, shall in the mean while be performed by the classis.

ART. XL.

The *deacons* shall likewise *meet together* every week in order to transact the business relating to their office, and shall open, and close their meeting with prayer. The minister shall carefully inspect their proceedings, and if necessary attend in person.

ART. XLI.

The *CLASSICAL ASSEMBLIES* shall be composed of neighbouring churches, each of which shall send one minister, and one elder, with proper credentials, to the place, and at the time agreed upon at the rising of the preceding classis; provided always, that the intervals between the classical meetings shall not exceed three months. In those assemblies the ministers shall preside in rotation, or otherwise a præses shall be appointed by the members, so that the same person however be not chosen twice successively. The præses shall moreover enquire of the members respectively, whether they observe their consistorial meetings? whether church discipline be exercised? whether the poor, and the schools are properly taken care of? and, whether they stand in need of the advice and assistance of the classis, in any thing respecting the regulation of their churches? The minister who was appointed by the last preceding classis, shall at the opening of the session deliver a sermon, of which the other members are to judge, and to point out its defects, if any there be. Lastly, the classis shall, at their meeting next preceding that of the particular synod, appoint Delegates to attend the said Synod.

The assumption behind this rule is that the classis ceases to exist between meetings. The understanding that any of the higher assemblies were "permanent and continuing bodies" is a later development. The Dutch Reformed emphasis on the absolute equality of all ministers (see Rules17 and 84) probably lies behind the prevention of any minister from presiding more than once.

ART. XLII.

In churches where there are more ministers than one, each minister shall have liberty to appear in the classis, and be entitled to a *deciding voice,* such cases excepted which particularly affect their persons, or congregations.

ART. XLIII.

At the close of the classical, and other higher assemblies a *censura morum* shall be held with respect to those who have been guilty of any censurable conduct in the assembly, or who have despised the admonitions of the lesser judicatories.

The Latin words *censura morum* simply mean a "censure of conduct," and it was a minimal type of mutual self-discipline within meetings. This rule was left out of the Church Order of 1833.

ART. XLIV.

Each classis shall authorize two or more of the eldest, most experienced, and best qualified of its members annually to *visit* all the churches belonging to its jurisdiction, both in the cities, and in the country; whose business it shall be to enquire, whether the ministers, consistories, and schoolmasters do faithfully discharge their offices? Whether they adhere to sound doctrine? Whether they observe, in all things, the received discipline, and promote, as much as possible, by word, and deed, the edification of the congregation in general, and of the youth in particular? That so they may seasonably, and in a brotherly manner, admonish those who in either of these particulars may be found negligent; and by their counsel, and conduct assist in directing all things to the edification, and prosperity of the churches, and schools.

Each Classis may continue their *Visitors* in office during pleasure, except when the visitors themselves for reasons, of which the classis shall judge request to be dismissed.

The system of *Visitors* and *Deputies* (see Rule 49) making personal visits was the Reformed church's most important means of ensuring unity, mutuality, pastoral care, and uniform discipline among the several congregations and respective assemblies. The official visitation of churches was taken seriously by both the Lutheran and Reformed movements, and they severely criticized the Roman hierarchical bishops for having failed to do it.

ART. XLV.

The churches in which either the classis, the particular, or general synod assembles, shall be careful to provide them with the *minutes* of the last preceding Assembly.

ART. XLVI.

Instructions respecting matters to be treated of in higher assemblies, are not to be recorded until the resolutions of the foregoing synod have been read, to the end that such things which have been determined, may not be again resumed, unless some alteration is conceived necessary.

ART. XLVII.

Once every year (unless an extraordinary session shall be judged necessary) two ministers, and two elders, delegated from four or more neighbouring classes, shall meet and constitute a *PARTICULAR SYNOD*. At the rising of every synod, the time, and place of their next meeting shall be ascertained.

The Dutch version states that each adjourning synod shall appoint a church to have the burden of determining, with the advice of classis, the time and place of the next meeting.

ART. XLVIII.

Every synod shall be at liberty to solicit, and hold *correspondence* with its neighbouring synod, or synods, in such manner as shall be judged most conducive to general edification.

ART. XLIX.

Every synod shall *depute* some of its members to put in

execution whatever has been ordained by such synod, as well in matters of a general concern, as in what relates to the respective classes in particular, that are subject to its jurisdiction; which *deputies*, or at least some of them, shall also be present at the examination of all candidates for the ministry; and shall moreover afford the classis their advice, and assistance in whatever difficulties may occur, to the end that uniformity, order, and purity of doctrine may be maintained, and established. They shall also keep a faithful record of their proceedings, that they may report the same to the synod, to whom they shall produce the reasons of their conduct, if thereunto required; nor shall they be dismissed from their commission, until the synod shall discharge them.

ART. L.

A *GENERAL SYNOD* shall be held ordinarily every three years (unless a pressing necessity shall require a shorter recess.) To this synod two ministers and two elders shall be delegated from every particular synod, both of the Dutch and Walloon churches. Moreover the church charged with nominating the time and place for the meeting of the general synod, in case of its being called together within three years, shall assemble the particular synod to which it belongs and give notice of the same to the next adjacent church that uses a different language, which church shall send thither four persons, in order with general consent, to fix upon a proper time and place.

The Dutch adds the following: "The same church that is chosen to call a meeting of the General Synod, when it consults with the Classis about the time and place, shall also give the Civil Authorities timely notice, so that, with their knowledge and (should it please them to send somebody to the Classis) in the presence of and with the advice of their Deputies they may conclude the matter." The Synod of Dort had assumed that there would be another national synod by 1622. For political reasons, it didn't happen (the unexpected delay lasted till 1816, when the government sponsored an "appointed" synod). It was a considerable step for the North American congregations to organize themselves into a General Synod in 1794, daring to do something that the mother church had been unable to do, and establishing a judicatory higher in rank than any in the Netherlands at the time.

ART. LI.

Whereas, two languages are used in the Netherlands, it is judged proper that the *Dutch and Walloon churches* shall have their distinct consistories, classical assemblies, and particular synods.

The Dutch Reformed church was bilingual from the beginning, having been born in what is now Belgium. After the division of the Netherlands it included in its ranks many Protestant refugees from Belgium and France. The very first communion service in Manhattan was conducted in both Dutch and French. There were a number of French congregations in the denomination during the whole colonial era, but by the 1790s there were too few to suggest a separate classis. Actually, at that time there were four languages in regular use in the Reformed church: Dutch, English, French, and German.

ART. LII.

It is notwithstanding judged proper that in those cities where the above mentioned *Walloon churches* are, some ministers, and elders of both descriptions should assemble together monthly, in order to preserve unity, and mutual good correspondence, and as much as possible, according to circumstances, with counsel to assist each other.

I I I.

O F

DOCTRINES, SACRAMENTS,

AND

USAGES.

ART. LIII.

The *MINISTERS* of the word of God, as also the *PROFESSORS* of theology, shall *subscribe* the confession of faith of the re- formed Church of the Netherlands, and ministers who refuse so to do, shall immediately be suspended from their service, either by the consistory, or by the classis, until they shall have fully explained themselves; and if they continue obstinate in their refusal, they shall be wholly deposed from the ministry.

ART. LIV.

In like manner shall the *Schoolmasters,* under the immediate care of the consistory, be obliged to *subscribe* the aforesaid articles, or instead thereof, the Heidelbergh catechism.

ART. LV.

No person professing the christian religion shall undertake to publish, or cause to be published any book, or writing on a religious subject, composed, or translated by himself, or another, without the previous inspection and *approbation* of the ministers of his Classis, or of the particular synod, or of the professors of theology in that province, with the consent of the classis.

This sort of rule was in Dutch church orders from the beginning and simply reflects a right that all churches used to claim, though we now associate it only the with Roman church.

ART. LVI.

The covenant of God shall be sealed by *Baptism,* to the infants of christians, in the public assembly, when the word of God is preached, and as early as the administration thereof can be obtained. In places where no stated service is performed, a certain day shall be appointed in the week, for the extraordinary celebration of baptism, but not without a sermon previously delivered.

This rule reflects the fact that, as late as 1619, it was still not everywhere taken for granted that baptism should take place within the ordinary public worship service, a principle goal of the Reformers. There is no explicit requirement that the elders rule on a request for baptism, or even that one of the parents must be a member in full communion.

ART. LVII.

The ministers shall exert their utmost endeavours that the *father* present his child to baptism, and in those congregations where it is customary, besides the father, to have *sponsors,* or witnesses, (which practice being in itself indifferent, is not causelessly to be altered) it is expedient that such only be admitted, as are sound in the faith and of exemplary lives.

This rule allows for godparents as a thing "indifferent," but disciplines the practice by, first, stipulating that the natural father present the child; second, signifying the godfather as chiefly a "witness"; and third, setting a high standard.

ART. LVIII.

Ministers in *baptising* infants, as well as adults, shall make use of the adopted *forms* in which the institution, and design of baptism, are for that purpose particularly explained.

The rule refers, of course, to *The Form for the Administration of Baptism, to Infants of Believers* and, appended to it, *The form for the Administration of Holy Baptism, to adult persons*, which are in the Liturgy. This rule testifies to the typical Reformed emphasis on the teaching function of the Liturgy. This is a catechetical approach to worship, though critics have called it merely a didactic approach.

ART. LIX.

Adults by baptism are initiated into the christian church, and received as members thereof in full communion, and therefore are bound to partake of the Lord's Supper, which they shall promise at their baptism.

This rule reflects the circumstance that many believers were reluctant to take Communion. Late medieval penitential piety had been transformed into a post-Reformation popular emphasis on "worthiness" and a fear of profaning the Lord's Table.

ART. LX.

A faithful *register* shall be kept of the names of all those who are baptized, and also of the parents, and witnesses, as well as of the time of baptism.

ART. LXI.

No person shall be admitted to the *Lord's supper*, but those who make a confession of their faith in the reformed religion, agreeably to the practice of the churches to which they are joined, and who also have the testimony of a pious deportment; without which also none coming from other churches, shall be received.

The Liturgy contains no form for "a confession of faith," since this was a private act done before the consistory.

ART. LXII.

Every church shall observe such a mode in *administering* the Lord's supper as shall be judged most conducive to edification; provided however, that the external ceremonies prescribed in the word of God, be not altered, and that all superstition be avoided. After the sermon, and usual public prayers are ended, the form for the administration of the Lord's supper, together with the prayer suited to the occasion, shall be read before the members approach the tables.

Earlier church orders gave some specific Communion rubrics in an effort to discipline left-over medieval practices, but this rule gives considerable freedom of mode so long as the *Form for the Administration of the LORD'S SUPPER* in the Liturgy is read. The Dutch Reformed practice was to celebrate by seating the communicants at large tables. The "usual public prayers" refers to the two *Prayers after sermon* which are also in the Liturgy. The Dutch original of this rule, however, specifically requires the minister to read the usual public prayers "from the pulpit," and to read the form and prayer for Communion "at the front of the table," that is, at the head of the long table at which people were seated.

ART. LXIII.

The Lord's supper shall be *celebrated* once every two months, if the same shall be convenient; and it will be expedient where the circumstances of the church admit, that it be administered at Easter, Whitsuntide, and Christmas. In places where no church is yet organised, elders, and deacons shall be previously appointed.

Whitsuntide is Pentecost. The recommendation to celebrate the great holidays of the Christian calendar by means of the Supper shows the effect of the Reformation's renovation of Communion. But over the following centuries, Good Friday, which is not even recognized in the Church Order, replaced Easter as the ordinary day for Communion. We do know from archival sources, however, that congregations were still celebrating Easter Communion in the 1790s. The phrase "if the same shall be convenient" could have been better translated as "whenever it is possible," and "previously appointed" should have been "provisionally appointed." The assumption of this stipulation is that, while a minister distributes the sacraments, it is a consistory that hosts Communion, and it therefore cannot be celebrated by a minister alone.

ART. LXIV.

As the *evening service* has been found beneficial in many places, every church shall be at liberty to adopt such measures in this respect as shall be judged most conducive to edification; but where such service has been customary, it shall not be laid aside without the approbation of classis.

The Dutch is literally "Evening Prayers" (*preces vespertinæ* in the Latin version), but the North American church took this rule to refer to the second service on the Lord's Day (see Rule 68).

ART. LXV.

In places where *funeral sermons* are not in use, they shall not be introduced; and where they have already obtained, endeavours shall be used to abolish them in the best manner possible.

The Dutch church was rigidly against church funerals and maintained that they were strictly private affairs (even though the wealthy were still buried beneath the church floor). The earliest versions of the Netherlands Liturgy did include a public funeral prayer, but in 1581 the National Synod of Middelburg ordered it removed.

ART. LXVI.

In times of war, pestilence, famine, severe persecutions of the church, and other general calamities, the ministers of the churches shall petition the civil rulers, that by their authority, and command, *days of public fasting, and prayer,* may be set apart, and sanctified.

The North American Synod did exactly this repeatedly in the decades between the American Revolution and the Civil War.

ART. LXVII.

Besides the sabbath day, the congregations shall likewise *observe* Christmas, Easter, and Whitsuntide, with the day succeeding each: and whereas in most of the cities, and provinces of the Netherlands, it is moreover customary to observe the day of the circumcision, and ascension of our Lord, the Ministers where such practice has not been adopted, shall endeavour to prevail with the civil authority to establish a conformity with the other churches.

As above, Whitsuntide is Pentecost. The "day of the Circumcision of Christ" is January 1. One effect of the Reformation was to simplify the church year, and some Calvinistic churches went so far as to abolish all holidays except Sunday, which they came to call "the Sabbath." The Provincial Synod of 1574 attempted to do the same in the Netherlands, but by 1619 the Dutch church had settled on maintaining, and even requiring, the major festivals that commemorated events in the life of Christ, and all five of them became civil holidays.

ART. LXVIII.

Every minister shall in the ordinary afternoon service on the Lord's day, briefly *explain* the system of the christian doctrine comprehended in *the catechism*, adopted by the reformed churches; so that if practicable, the explanation may be annually completed, according to the sections made for that purpose in said catechism.

The Heidelberg Catechism was intended to be taught not only in the classroom but also from the pulpit, and for this purpose it was divided into fifty-two "Lord's Days." This rule mandates the second service on the Lord's Day (the origin of the Sunday evening service) as a catechetical service (*leerdienst*). The Liturgy includes pulpit *Prayers before and after Catechism*.

ART. LXIX.

The 150 *psalms* of David; the ten commandments; the Lord's prayer; the 12 articles of the christian faith; the *songs* of Mary, Zachariah, and Simeon versified, only, shall be sung in public worship. The churches are left at liberty to adopt, or omit that entitled, "*O thou, who art our Father God!*" All others are prohibited, and where any have been already introduced, they shall be discontinued as soon as possible.

This rule stipulates the exclusive use of the Genevan Psalter,

that most characteristic symbol of Reformed worship. It was
available in many languages, including French, German, and
Dutch. The New-York Consistory had sponsored an English
version of it, which proved defective. In 1789 the North American
Synod published its own English psalter, which, however, was
based on the Anglican "New Version" and did not make use of the
Genevan tunes. The one extra-biblical hymn, "O God, die onsen
Vader bist," came into Dutch Reformed worship by way of the
Liturgy of Dathenus, where it was appended to the *Prayer before
Sermon on the Lord's Day*. The hymn was made optional in 1574.

ART. LXX.

In matters relating to *matrimony,* the churches shall abide by
those usages, which they have hitherto observed, conformably
to the word of God, and former ecclesiastical ordinances, at least
until the civil government shall institute some general ordinance
for that purpose.

The Liturgy contains a *Form for the Confirmation of Marriage,
before the Church.*

IV.

OF

CHRISTIAN

DISCIPLINE

ARTICLE LXXI.

As *CHRISTIAN DISCIPLINE* is spiritual, and exempts no person
from the judgment and punishment of the civil power, so it is

requisite that without any reference to civil punishment, ecclesiastical, or spiritual censure should be exercised, in order to reconcile the delinquent with the church, and with his neighbour, and that offences may be removed out of the church of Christ.

Christian discipline was taken seriously by the Reformed church. Article 29 of the Belgic Confession calls it one of the three marks of the church, and Answers 83 and 85 of the Heidelberg Catechism call it one of the two "Keys of the Kingdom of Heaven." The Dutch practice of church discipline evolved over seven decades, beginning in 1552 with the Church Order of the Dutch congregation in London (published in 1554 as Micron's *Christlicke Ordinancien*), passing through the tinkering of successive provincial and national synods, and culminating in 1619 with the Rules of the Synod of Dort. This rule jealously affirms the right of church discipline to be independent of the civil power (though complementary to it), which right was not taken for granted at the time.

ART. LXXII.

When *any person offends* either against purity of doctrine, or of morals, and such offence is *private*, and has given rise to no public scandal; in such case the method shall be pursued which is pointed out by our Lord, in the 18th chapter of Matthew.

The passage from Matthew, in a contemporary King James Version, is as follows:

Moreover, if thy brother shall trespass against thee, go and tell him his fault between thee and him alone; if he shall hear thee, thou hast gained thy brother. But if he will not hear thee, then take with thee one or two more, that in the mouth of two or three witnesses every word may be established. And if he shall neglect to hear them, tell it unto the church: but if he neglect to hear the church, let him be unto thee as an heathen man and a publican. Verily, I say unto you, Whatsoever ye shall bind on earth, shall be bound in heaven: and whatsoever ye shall loose on earth, shall be loosed in heaven.

ART. LXXIII.

Secret sins shall not be brought before the Consistory, when the offender has discovered proofs of repentance, on being admonished by a single person in private, or before two, or three witnesses.

ART. LXXIV.

If any person guilty of a private offence shall reject the friendly admonition given him before two, or three witnesses, or shall have committed a *crime publickly known*, the same shall be reported to the Consistory.

ART. LXXV.

The *satisfaction* for such offences, which are in their own nature public, or are become notorious by the contempt of ecclesiastical admonitions, shall, when evident proofs of repentance are given, be made in a public manner, at the discretion of the Consistory. In the country, and in villages where there is but one minister, the satisfaction shall be made with the advice of two neighbouring Churches, in such manner and form as shall appear most edifying.

The word *satisfaction* translates the Dutch word *verzoening*, which more strictly means *reconciliation* or *atonement*.

ART. LXXVI.

Such as obstinately reject the admonitions of the Consistory, or have committed a public, or otherwise gross offence, shall be *suspended* from the Lord's supper; and being suspended, and repeatedly admonished, without discovering marks of repentance, the church shall then proceed to the last remedy, namely, *Excommunication*, agreeably to the adopted form, and conformably to the word of God. But no person shall be excommunicated without the previous advice of the Classis.

The *Form of Excommunication* is part of the Liturgy. The form also outlines the procedure stipulated in these rules.

ART. LXXVII.

Before the church proceeds to Excommunication, the obstinacy of the offender shall be publicly notified to the congregation, declaring his offences, together with the particular care, and attention bestowed on him, by admonition, suspension from the Lord's table, and by repeated remonstrances. The congregation shall also be exhorted farther to admonish the delinquent, and to pray for him. This procedure shall be comprised in three several steps. In the *first* instance, the name of the offender shall not be mentioned that he may in some measure be spared. In the *second* with the advice of Classis his name shall be expressed. In the *third* the congregation shall be informed that unless he repenteth, he will be excluded from the communion of the church; so that if he remain obstinate, his excommunication may take place with their tacit approbation. The interval between these notifications shall be at the discretion of the Consistory.

ART. LXXVIII.

When an excommunicated person becomes *penitent*, and is desirous of being again reconciled to the church, such desire shall be publicly declared to the congregation either before the administration of the Lord's supper, or at some other seasonable opportunity that if no objections are offered, he may on declaring his repentance, be publicly readmitted to a participation of the Lord's supper, agreeably to the form appointed for that purpose.

The Form of readmitting excommunicated persons into the church of Christ is in the Liturgy.

ART. LXXIX.

If *Ministers* of the word, *Elders* or *Deacons* have committed any public gross sin, which is scandalous to the church, or punishable by the civil magistrate; the elders, or deacons shall immediately be removed from their office by the previous determination of the consistory of their own, and next adjacent church. But the ministers shall be suspended, and it shall be left to the decision of the classis whether they shall be wholly deposed, or not.

Consistories have full jurisdiction over elders and deacons. They have only temporary jurisdiction over ministers, whose cases are automatically remanded to the classis. Consistories do have the right to protect themselves from their own ministers until their classis decides the case. The following rule concerns office-bearers as opposed to "private" or lay members.

ART. LXXX.

The following are to be considered as the *principal offences* that deserve the punishment of suspension, or removal from office, viz. False Doctrine or Heresy, public Schisms, open Blasphemy, Simony, faithless desertion of his Office, or intruding upon that of another, Perjury, Adultery, Fornication, Theft, acts of Violence, Brawlings, habitual Drunkenness, and scandalous Traffick; in short all such sins, and gross offences which render the perpetrators infamous before the world, and which in a private member of the church would be considered as deserving excommunication.

ART. LXXXI.

The ministers, elders, and deacons shall exercise *Christian Discipline amongst themselves*, and exhort one another in a friendly manner respecting the discharge of their offices.

ART. LXXXII.

The minister with the approbation of monsistory shall furnish those members who remove out of the congregation with a *certificate* of their behaviour, sealed with the seal of the church, or where there is no seal, signed by the minister, or by two of the elders.

ART. LXXXIII.

When *Indigent Members* for sufficient reasons remove out of the congregation, they shall be assisted by the deacons in such measure, as they shall think proper; taking care, however, that the place to which they are going, and the assistance which has been afforded them be endorsed upon their testimonials.

ART. LXXXIV.

No church shall exercise *authority* over another, nor any minister over his brethren in the ministry, nor shall elders and deacons rule over other elders and deacons.

When more than one minister served a single congregation, they shared everything equally in rotation, and no such thing as "senior pastor" or "assistant pastor" was allowed. The Dutch cities had a single consistory supervising all the local congregations, in the "collegiate" pattern. There might be as many as twenty ministers in consistory, and all were held strictly equal.

ART. LXXXV.

In things indifferent, *foreign churches* shall not be rejected whose customs, and usages vary from ours.

The Dutch church distinguished between essentials and "things indifferent" (*adiaphora, middelmaatige dingen*). Thus, French, German, and English congregations were permitted to belong to the Reformed church and maintain peculiarities in worship and government. This freedom was limited to Reformed groups, however.

ART. LXXXVI.

These articles relating to the regular government of the church, have been formed, and adopted by common consent in such manner, that if the interest of the church should require it, they may and ought to be altered, enlarged, or diminished; this however, shall not be attempted by any particular congregation, classis, or synod, but, on the contrary, a careful observance of them is enjoined until it be otherwise ordained by a succeeding general, or national synod.

Because the Dutch government refused to call another national synod in the decades after 1619, the rules could not be amended, and the Church Order eventually came to be seen as something unchanging. Not till after the Napoleonic Wars and the reconstitution of the Dutch nation was the Church Order altered in any way, and then in 1816 it was changed radically, becoming the *Algemeen Reglement*.

The preceding ecclesiastical ordinances were made and decreed in the national synod, held at Dordrecht the 28th. day of May, in the year 1619.

And were signed,

JOHANNES BOGERMANNUS, Synodi Præses.
JACOBUS ROLANDUS, Assessor.
HERMANUS FAUKELIUS, Præsidis Assessor.
SEBASTIANUS DAMMON, Synodi Scriba.
FESTUS HOMMIUS, Synodi Scriba.

AT A CONVENTION of Ministers and Elders delegated for the express purpose of removing certain difficulties, which had arisen in the Reformed Dutch Churches in America, and for establishing an uniform discipline throughout the same, held at New-York, in the month of October, 1771, the Rules of Church Government, made and decreed in the National Synod, held at Dordrecht, 1618 and 1619, were recognised, and expressly adopted as the Constitution of the said churches, as far as their local circumstances would render the same practicable.

The Articles of Union founded upon this adoption, and expressing in general terms what is specified, and more particularly applied to the local circumstances of the churches, in the following Explanatory Articles, were ratified and established on the 18th day of October, 1771.

And were signed,

JOHN H. LIVINGSTON, Præses.
ISAAC RYSDYCK, Scriba.
EILARDUS WESTERLO, Scriba.

ARTICLES

EXPLANATORY

OF THE

GOVERNMENT and DISCIPLINE

OF THE

REFORMED DUTCH CHURCH,

IN THE

UNITED STATES

OF

AMERICA.

WHEREAS *the Rules of Church Government, commonly called the* Church Orders, *which were ratified in the National Synod held at Dordrecht in the years* 1618, *and* 1619, *and which express the general principles of Ecclesiastical government adopted by all reformed churches; were, by the delegates from the United Netherlands,* explained *and more fully* applied *to their local circumstances, in certain acts, which were stiled the* Post Acta Synodi Nationalis.

AND WHEREAS *the reformed Dutch churches in America, who brought with them from Holland the discipline established in the National Synod of Dordrecht, have also, always* applied *the same, as far as their numbers, and situation would permit; and in a general convention of delegates held at New-York, in the year of our Lord* 1771, *did declare their firm adherance to the Ecclesiastical ordinances aforesaid, in the first article of their acts then ratified, in the words following, viz.* "*We abide fully by the constitution of the reformed church of the Netherlands, as the same is established in the National Synod held at Dordrecht, Annis* 1618, *and* 1619."

AND WHEREAS, *it is judged proper to publish the government and discipline of the reformed Dutch church in America, in the English language, and it is thereby become necessary, not only to translate the Rules of Church Government of the National Synod of Dordrecht, but also to* explain *in what manner the said rules are executed, consistant with the local circumstances of said church.*

THEREFORE, *the General Synod of the reformed Dutch church in America, held at New-York, in October* 1792, *have caused the practice of their church to be comprised in the following* EXPLAN-ATORY ARTICLES, *agreeably to which, the Rules of Church Government of the said National Synod of Dordrecht are applied and executed.*

EXPLANATORY ARTICLES.

I.

OF THE

OFFICES IN THE CHURCH.

I.

MINISTERS OF THE WORD.

ART. I.

No person can be chosen or called to be a Minister of the Word, who has not previously become a *candidate* for the ministry.

The first twelve articles regulate the preparation of candidates for the Ministry. In the Netherlands it was the universities which governed the preparation of candidates and presented them to the respective classes. Lacking a national system of university regulations in America, the synod had to have its own. The first article introduces *candidate* as a technical term of the Constitution. The two following articles define the educational process. In the background of this is the Coetus and Conferentie schism, when one side accused the other of irregularly ordaining uneducated and unqualified men. Rule 7 in the Church Order, which allows for extraordinary ordinations of uneducated persons, is not addressed by these articles, thereby allowing for the possibility without necessarily encouraging it.

ART. II.

A candidate for the ministry is one, who, after finishing his Theological studies, has submitted to a public examination; and, upon being found well qualified, is licenced to preach the gospel, and permitted to accept a call in any congregation.

This article mandates the "Examination for Licensure," which the Reformed church still requires today. Until 1833 the examination could be conducted by a synod as well as by a classis, thereafter only by a classis.

ART. III.

Whoever applies to be examined for becoming a candidate in the ministry, must produce to the Synod, or Classis to which the application is made, the following authentic documents: 1. A diploma, or certificate of his having passed through a regular course of studies in some College or respectable Academy. 2. A certificate of his having been a member in full commumion of the reformed Church, at least two years. And 3. A testimonial under the hand and seal of a Professor of Theology, declaring such student to have studied Theology with him (or with some person expressly authorised for that purpose by the General Synod,) for the space of at least two years; and recommending said student as well qualified for becoming a candidate in the holy ministry.

This article mandates the "Professorial Certificate" which, until 1985, all seminary graduates had to receive in order to admit them to the Examination for Licensure. This has now been replaced by the Certificate of Fitness for Ministry.

ART. IV.

In the examination, strict attention is paid to the attainments of the Student, not only in the original languages of the sacred Scriptures, and in composition, and his method of sermonizing; but he is especially examined respecting his knowledge in Theology, his orthodoxy, his piety, and his views in desiring to become a preacher of the gospel.

ART. V.

Whoever, upon examination, shall be approved by the Synod or Classis, must, before he is licensed, attest his adherence to the doctrines of the gospel, by subscribing the following formula, viz.

"WE the underwritten, testify, that the Heidelbergh Catechism, and the confession of the Netherland Churches; as also the Canons of the National Synod of Dordrecht, held in the years 1618 and 1619, are fully comformable to the word of God. We promise moreover, that as far as we are able, we will, with all faithfulness, teach and defend both in public and private, the doctrines established in the standards aforesaid. And, should it ever happen that any part of these doctrines appear to us dubious, that we will not divulge the same to the people, nor disturb the peace of the Church or of any community, until we first communicate our sentiments to the ecclesiastical Judicatories under which we stand, and subject ourselves to the council and sentence of the same."

The Form of Subscription for Licensed Candidates was apparently newly written for the Explanatory Articles. It is clearly derived from the form of Subscription for Ministers (Article XI). The form evolved into the modern Declaration for Licensed Candidates now found in the Formularies.

ART. VI.

After subscribing the aforesaid formula, the candidate is entitled to a certificate, or testimonial signed by the President of the Synod, or classis, before whom the examination is held, containing a license to preach the Gospel, and recommending his person and services to the Churches.

ART. VII.

A candidate for the ministry is permitted only to preach the word, but he may not under any pretence whatever, administer the sacraments; nor can he be a delegate to represent a Church in any ecclesiastical assembly.

ART. VIII.

Every candidate for the Ministry is to consider himself under the immediate direction of the Synod, and the classis which examined him, and is to visit such congregations, and preach in those places to which the Synod, or classis shall send him: but if no particular directions are given, he may preach at his own discretion in any congregation that shall invite him.

ART. IX.

Upon receiving a call from any particular congregation, a candidate is allowed time to consider the propriety of his accepting it. If more than one call is before him at the same time, he may determine which he will prefer; but if there be only one, it is expected he will not finally refuse the same, before having first referred his difficulties to the Synod, or classis, and obtained proper advice.

ART. X.

A candidate who has accepted a call, must offer himself to be examined for his becoming a Minister. In this final examination, besides a repetition of his previous trials in composition and sermonizing, the original languages of the sacred scriptures, and his knowledge of Theology, as well didactic and as polemic; he is interrogated respecting the nature, and administration of the sacraments, the duties of the Ministry, and his knowledge of ecclesiastical history, and of Church government.

This article mandates a second and more comprehensive examination. This is actually the classical examination required by Rule 4 of Dort. It must be remembered that the first examination in the articles above is an American substitute for Dutch university exams. With the classis doing both of them, the first

examination began to take on the weight of the second one, and
the second examination of a fully licensed candidate in possession
of a call has become strictly optional, and quite rare.

ART. XI.

Upon giving satisfaction in the examination, the candidate
subscribes the following formula, viz.

"WE the underwritten, Ministers of the word of God, residing
within the bounds of the Classis of N. N. do hereby sincerely, and
in good conscience before the Lord, declare by this our
subscription, that we heartily believe and are persuaded, that all
the articles and points of doctrine contained in the Confession
and Catechism of the reformed Dutch Church, together with the
explanation of some points of the aforesaid doctrine made in the
national Synod, held at Dordrecht, in the year 1619, do fully
agree with the word of God. We promise therefore, diligently to
teach, and faithfully to defend the aforesaid doctrine, without
either directly or indirectly contradicting the same by our public
preaching or writings. We declare moreover, that we not only
reject all errors that militate against this doctrine, and particularly
those which are condemned in the above mentioned Synod; but
that we are disposed to refute and contradict them, and to exert
ourselves in keeping the Church pure from such errors. And if
hereafter any difficulties, or different sentiments respecting the
aforesaid doctrine should arise in our minds, we promise, that we
will neither publicly nor privately, propose, teach or defend the
same, either by preaching or writing, until we have first revealed
such sentiment to the consistory, classis, and Synod, that the
same may be there examined; being ready always, cheerfully to
submit to the judgment of the consistory, classis, or Synod, under
the penalty, in case of refusal, to be *ipso facto* suspended from
our office. And further, if at any time the consistory, the classis or
Synod, upon sufficient grounds of suspicion, and to preserve the

uniformity and purity of doctrine, may deem it proper to require of us a farther explanation of our sentiments, respecting any particular article of the Confession of Faith, the Catechism, or the explanation of the national Synod, we do hereby promise to be always willing and ready to comply with such requisition, under the penalty abovementioned; reserving however to ourselves the right of an appeal, whenever we shall conceive ourselves aggrieved by the sentence of the consistory, the classis, or particular Synod; and until a decision is made upon such appeal, we will acquiesce in the determination and judgment already passed."

This article mandates the Form of Subscription for Ministers, and enters the text of it into the constitution. The form is a fair translation of the Dutch original. The form was drafted at the Synod of Dort, and ratified at Session 164, although it was never included in the Church Order of Dort *per se*. It was part of the document called the "Post-Acta," the nondoctrinal and practical decisions made by the Dutch delegates after all the international delegates went home. The form was readily available in the *Kerkelyk Hantboekje*. The form has evolved over the years, and with some controversy, into the "Declaration for Ministers" in the modern Formularies.

ART. XII.

Upon subscribing the aforesaid formula, a certificate, signed by the President shall be given to the candidate; and the Synod, or classis, before which the examination is held, shall fix a day for his ordination, and name at least three Ministers to attend, and assist at the same.

ART. XIII.

The ordination shall be conducted with proper solemnity. A sermon suited to the occasion shall be preached by him who is named the moderator for that purpose; and the promises, directions, explanations of duty, with the laying on of hands, shall be agreeably to the form for that end expressly made and adopted.

ART. XIV.

Every Minister must consider himself as wholly devoted to the Lord Jesus Christ in the service of the Church; and shall faithfully fulfil the obligations of his call, in preaching, catechising, and visiting his flock; and be instant in season and out of season; and by word and example always promote the spiritual welfare of his people.

Article XIII expands on Rule 4, point 4, of Dort. Article XIV requires that ministers be "full-time." This was taken for granted in the Netherlands, but frontier conditions in America had sometimes required otherwise.

ART. XV.

All the Ministers and Elders, regularly deputed, shall punctually attend the judicatories of which they are members; and for repeated neglect shall be subject to a reprimand, or such other censure as shall be judged proper; and their respective congregations are to consider themselves bound to afford them the opportunity of attendance.

ART. XVI.

Ministers, who by reason of old age, or habitual sickness and infirmities, either of mind or body, are not capable of fulfilling the duties of the Ministry, may, upon application, and sufficient proof of such incapacity being made to the Classis, be declared Emeriti, and be excused from all further service in the Church during such infirmity; reserving however to them, the title, rank, and character, which before such declaration they enjoyed. In all such cases, the Classis shall make it a condition previous to any Minister's becoming emeritus, that the congregation enter into stipulations obliging them to a reasonable, and annual support to their pastor who has grown old, or become sick and infirm in their service.

ART. XVII.

Ministers declared emeriti, shall be amenable to the judicatories to which they belong, but they may not proceed to the administration of the Sacraments, or celebration of marriage, while they continue emeriti, unless expressly permitted by the Classis.

Articles XVI and XVII expand on Rule 13 of Dort. The financial support of disabled or retired ministers was hardly a problem in the Netherlands, with its excellent welfare system and the church established. But this was not the case in America, and the synod had to address it. At the same time, retired pastors were prevented from picking up a few extra dollars by performing pastoral acts at the expense of their successors.

ART. XVIII.

All Ministers of the gospel are equal in rank and authority; all are Bishops, or Overseers in the Church; and all are equally Stewards of the mysteries of God. No superiority shall therefore be ever claimed or acknowledged by one Minister over another, nor shall there be any Lords over God's heritage in the reformed Dutch Churches.

This article interprets Rules 17 and 84 of Dort. It is a remarkable item, evidencing the *confessional* character of the whole constitution. While, in the Netherlands, the Reformed church had no real competitors, in North America the Dutch church found itself between two much larger Protestant competitors, the Episcopalians and the Presbyterians. With an eye on its distinctions from both, and borrowing terminology from the *Ordination Form* in the Liturgy, it claims the title *bishop* for local pastors, while at the same time it stoutly denies any hierarchy in the church. This article avoids both Anglicanism with its prelatical view of bishops and American Presbyterianism with its collapsing of all the offices into the eldership. The Belgic Confession, Articles 30 and 31, teaches the permanent three-fold offices of minister, elder, and deacon, as do most of the early Reformed church orders (including the Church of Scotland), equating the office of the local pastor with that of the bishop. See also the Latin footnote to the next article.

II.

PROFESSORS OF THEOLOGY

ART. XIX.

The distinction between the first and second office in the church, that is, between the Ministers of the word and Teachers of Theology, is founded in the nature of the respective offices. The former are those, who by preaching and ruling, instruct, and govern the church; and are, as such, denominated pastors or shepherds of the flock: the latter are those who are set apart only to teach and defend the truths of the Gospel, and for that reason, are excused from fulfilling the pastoral duties. This distinction was noted in the early ages of the christian church.* It was attended to at the reformation, and was productive of important benefits, especially with respect to the education of candidates for the holy Ministry. The reformed Dutch Church perseveres in preserving the same distinction, and determines that the instructing, and preparing youth for the service of the sanctuary, shall not be left indiscriminately to every Minister, or any individual who may choose to assume that office.

Pastores ac doctores. Assentior Ambrosio, qui haec quoque munera distinguit; nam ratio parum firma est quae Hieronymum, et Augustinum movit ut confunderent, nempe, quia copula duntaxit est interjecta. Fateor tamen Doctorum nomen late patere, ut I. Cor. xii. Sed tamen apparet aliquod fuisse discrimen, quod in isto Compendio videtur vix locus esse synonymis. *Doctoris* igitur munus fuit verbum Domini fideliter explicare, et veluti Scholam ecclesiasticam regere, ut sincera doctrina dogmatum, et verae interpretationes in ecclesia retinerentur, sicut docuit Alexandriae Origines, ut explicatur Niceph. lib. Eccles. hist. v. Cap. 14. At *Pastorum* (qui et *Episcopi* dicebantur, ut I Pet. iii.) Munus longe latius patebat, nimirum verbo et oratione vacare, et Ecclesiam sibi commissam modis omnibus tueri: Exquibus etiam satis perspicitur haec duo munera perpetua esse oportere in Ecclesia Dei. Beza in Eps. ad Ephes. vi. 11.

This and the following six articles interpret Rule 18 of Dort. In the Netherlands the professorate belonged to the universities and was regulated thereby. In America, during the colonial era, there had been attempts to connect a Dutch Reformed theological professorate with either Princeton or King's (now Columbia). The controversies arising therefrom led the synod of 1784 finally to establish the professor strictly as an officer of the church, independent of any existing college, from which act the Theological Seminary of the Reformed church (now at New Brunswick) dates its birth.

The Latin footnote to this article is a quotation from Theodorus Beza's commentary on Ephesians (chapter 4 verse 11, not chapter 6), and it may be translated as follows: "*Pastors and teachers.* I agree with Ambrose, who also separated these two offices; since the argument that led Jerome and Augustine to combine

them—that the conjunction is merely thrown in—is not very
solid. I admit that the term Teacher is used broadly, as in I
Corinthians 12, but nevertheless there appears to have been some
distinction, because the placement in that compendium hardly
seems to be of synonyms. Therefore the office of *Teacher* is to
explain the Word of the Lord faithfully, and to rule the church as
a School, that sound doctrine is taught, and true interpretations
are held in the church, as Origen of Alexandria taught, as is
explained by Nicephorus in his Ecclesiastical History, book V,
chapter 14. And the office of *Pastors* (who are also called *Bishops*,
as in I Pet. 3) extends more broadly, to devote himself wholly to
the word and prayer, and to care in all ways for the Church
entrusted to him; from which it is clear enough that these two
offices should remain permanently in the Church of God." Beza,
On the Epistle to the Ephesians, vi. 11.

ART. XX.

Professors of Theology, have, as such, no power, jurisdiction, or
government whatever in the Church; but as they are Ministers
who preach occasionally, they are entitled, when they stand in
connection with any Congregation, equally with other Ministers,
to administer the sacraments, and to a seat and voice in
ecclesiastical assemblies.

The relative poverty of the church required the first professors,
Livingston of New York and Hermanus Meyer of Totowa, also to
serve as local pastors. In 1810 the professorate moved from New
York City to New Brunswick, and Livingston gave up his pastoral
charge in order to be the first full-time professor. Not until the
synod of 1819 was it ruled that professors might not also serve a
local congregation.

ART. XXI.

As it is of the last importance that Professors of Theology should
be sound in the faith, posess abilities to teach, and have the

confidence of the Churches, they shall always, for the greater security, be chosen and appointed by a majority of votes in the general Synod only. To prevent as far as possible the unhappy consequences of partiality, haste, or undue influence in obtaining an office of such consequence to the Church, a nomination of one, or more candidates shall be previously made, upon which the Synod shall fix a day when they will proceed to an election; provided that no appointment of a Professor in Theology shall ever be made on the same day in which he is nominated.—An instrument certifying the appointment, and specifying the duties of the office, shall be signed in the presence of the General Synod, by the president thereof, and by him be given, in the name of the Church, to the person elected.

The professors in the Netherlands were elected by the provincial synods. This article gives the prerogative to the General Synod only. At the time all nominations were made from the floor, which is why the article mandates a waiting period.

ART. XXII.

No professor of Theology shall be permitted to officiate, until he shall have subscribed the following formula, viz.

"WE, the underwritten, Professors of sacred Theology in the reformed Dutch Church, by this our subscription, uprightly, and in good conscience before God declare, that we heartily believe and are persuaded, that all the articles and points of doctrine contained in the Confession and Catechism of the reformed Dutch Churches, together with the explanation of some points of the said doctrine made in the national Synod held at Dordrecht in the year 1619, do fully agree with the word of God. We promise therefore, that we will diligently teach, and faithfully defend the aforesaid doctrine; and that we will not inculcate or write, either publicly or privately, directly or indirectly any thing against the same. As also, that we reject not only all the errors which militate against this doctrine, and particularly those which are condemned in the above mentioned Synod; but that we are disposed to refute the same, openly to oppose them, and to exert ourselves in keeping the church pure from such errors. Should it, nevertheless, hereafter happen, that any objections against the doctrine might arise in our minds, or we entertain different sentiments, we promise that we will not either publicly or privately propose, teach or defend the same by preaching or writing, until we have first fully revealed such sentiments to the General Synod, to whom we are responsible; that our opinions may in the said general Synod receive a thorough examination, being ready always cheerfully to submit to the judgment of the General Synod, under the penalty, in case of refusal, to be censured by the said Synod. And whenever the General Synod, upon sufficient grounds of suspicion, and to preserve the uniformity and purity of doctrines, may deem it proper to demand from us a more particular explanation of our sentiments any article of the aforesaid confession, catechism or explanation of the National Synod, we promise hereby to be always willing and ready to comply with such demand, under the penalty before mentioned; reserving to ourselves, the right of rehearing, or a new trial, if we shall conceive ourselves aggrieved in the sentence of the General Synod: during the dependance of which new trial, we promise to acquiesce in the judgment already passed, as well as finally to submit, without disturbing the peace of the churches, to the ultimate decision of the said General Synod."

The Form of Subscription for Professors of Theology could be found in the Post-Acta of Dort, under Session 175. It is a fair translation of the Dutch, although "Provincial Synod" and "Synod" have been changed to "General Synod" throughout. It is, naturally, very similar to the form for ministers. It was apparently little observed in the Netherlands, except at the University of Groningen.[9] It has evolved into our present "Declaration for

Professors of Theology," in the Formularies.

ART. XXIII.

As no student can be admitted to a public examination before any classis or synod, unless he shall produce a document under the hand and seal of a professor of theology, appointed by the general Synod; (See expl. art. 3.) so it shall be the duty of every professor, after repeated private examinations, faithfully and impartially, to certify the progress and attainments of every student, who has attended the lectures of the said professor for two years, or may have studied the same term, under some person for that purpose expressly named by the general Synod, and who shall apply to such professor for a certificate, and recommendation. All regulations respecting any further term for study, or any particular dispensation, which peculiar circumstances may render necessary in the case of any students in Theology shall be formed by the general Synod alone; to which, as well the professors, as the classes or particular synods shall submit, and always conform themselves.

This article further elaborates on the Professorial Certificate already mandated in Article III. It also introduces the option of the "Dispensation from the Professorial Certificate," and reserves the granting of this solely to the General Synod, not the classis. Since 1985 this has been called the "Dispensation from the Certificate of Fitness for Ministry."

ART. XXIV.

Every Professor of theology shall continue in his office during life, unless in case of such misbehaviour as shall be deemed a violation of the obligations entered into at his appointment; or unless he voluntarily deserts or resigns his profession; or from age or infirmities becomes incapable of fulfilling the duties thereof; of all which the general Synod alone shall judge; and to that Synod a Professor of Theology shall always be amenable for his doctrine, mode of teaching and moral conduct.

This article removes the professor from amenability to a local consistory, classis, or particular synod. The Church Order had been ambiguous on this, and certain intepretations held that, in spite of the professor's election by a particular synod and subscription with it, *every* officer of the church remained amenable to a consistory. This is the view that came to prevail in the Christian Reformed church. The 1793 synod obviously took it the other way, leading to one of the distinct differences between the Reformed and Christian Reformed denominations.

ART. XXV.

The general Synod will endeavor to procure and preserve a proper fund for the support of the professorship of theology; that the persons set apart for that office, may not be dependant upon any particular congregation, while they are employed for the common benefit of all the churches.

This article makes the General Synod directly responsible for financing theological education. Eventually, in the next century, as endowments were built up for the increasing number of professors, the finances of the seminary were separated from that of the synod.

III.

ELDERS and DEACONS

ART. XXVI.

The manner of chusing elders, and deacons, is not rigidly defined: A double number may be nominated by the consistory, out of which the members of the Church may choose those who shall serve.—Or, all the members may unite in nominating and choosing the whole number without the interference of the consistory.—or, the Consistory, for the time being, as representing all the members, may choose the whole, and refer the persons thus chosen, by publishing them in the church, for the approbation of the people. This last method has been found most convenient, especially in large churches, and has long been generally adopted. But where that, or either of the other modes has for many years been followed in any church, there shall be no variation or change, but by previous application to the classis, and express leave first obtained for altering such custom.

This article expands Rule 22 of Dort by adding the alternative of completely open nominations. But both the rule and article prefer the consistory to have a strong say in choosing their successors (with the endorsement of the congregation). The modern Church Order no longer suggests this, but it still requires that the manner of election not be changed without previous application to classis. Elders and deacons were not required to sign a form of subscription. The Synod of Dort, in Session 175 of the Post-Acta, had decided to leave the subscription of elders and deacons up to the discretion of the classes.

ART. XXVII.

The elders with the ministers of the word, constitute what the Reformed Dutch Church properly calls, the Consistory. But as the deacons have always in America, where the congregations were at first very small, (See Synod Dord. Art. 38.) been joined with the Elders, and wherever charters have been obtained, are particularly named, as forming with them one consistory, it is necessary to define their joint as well as respective powers. From the form of their ordination it is evident, that to the elders, together with the ministers of the word, is committed the spiritual government of each church; while to the deacons belong the obtaining charitable assistance and the distribution of the same in the most effectual manner for the relief and comfort of the poor. When joined together in one board, the elders and Deacons have all an equal voice in whatever relates to the temporalities of the church, to the calling of a minister, or the choice of their own successors; in all which, they are considered as the general and joint representatives of the people: but in admitting members to full communion; in exercising discipline upon those who have erred from the faith, or offended in morals; and in chusing delegates to attend the classis, the elders, with the ministers, have alone a voice.

Notwithstanding, as most of the consistories still remain small, it is resolved that the respective powers may remain blended; and the elders, and deacons continue to unite in executing the joint rights of a consistory respecting all the objects of the respective offices as hitherto they have done; and no change in any congregation shall in this matter be introduced, without first making application for that purpose to the classis, and obtaining an express regulation for the distinct and separate administration of the respective powers of the elders and deacons.

As many difficulties are known to have arisen in the minds of deacons, respecting the application of monies collected by them in the churches, to any other purposes than those of immediate charity; it becomes necessary to explain this subject, and remove the difficulties, by declaring that, the design and object of the collections are not only the relief of the poor, but also the necessities of the congregation. Charity extends to the souls of men as well as their bodies; and procuring the gospel for the poor is the highest benefit. If the abilities of the congregation therefore, are not adequate to the building of a church, or maintaining a minister, by means of subscription, or any other fund, there is no doubt, but the deacons may, in good conscience assist from their collections, and bestow as much as can be spared from the immediate wants of the suffering poor. Finally, as the deacons in every church are to be considered as serving the church, so they are in that service, subordinate to the rule and government of the church which is vested in the Consistory, (See Art. 25, of Syn. Dord.) and they ought to submit to the advice and direction of the same. But where no particular directions interfere, the deacons must proceed agreeably to their own discretion.

This is one of the longest of the articles. It explains why deacons are ordinarily part of American consistories, while in the Netherlands they are not. It goes on to delineate and distinguish from each other the duties of each office, as well as mention which powers the offices can equally share within the consistory. The article adds a significant paragraph of great importance to the free church environment of America. In the Netherlands, since the Reformed church was established, the government paid for its ordinary expenses, and the deacons were simply responsible for collecting funds for charity to the poor, especially to the widows and orphans. But now the church was disestablished, a contingency unseen by Dort. The general assumption was that endowments and subscriptions (pledges) would cover the usual expenses, but some congregations were coming up short. This article provides a somewhat tendentious apology for the necessity of deacons to divert their funds for the maintenance of the congregation. There was little choice. The unfortunate consequence of this, however, together with the acceptance of deacons into the consistory, was that the diaconate in the Reformed church gradually lost the heart of its original vocation.

ART. XXVIII.

In order to lessen the burthen of a perpetual attendance upon ecclesiastical duties, and by a rotation in office to bring forward deserving members, it is the established custom, in the reformed Dutch Church, that elders and deacons remain only two years in service, after which they retire from their respective offices, and others are chosen in their places; the rotation being always conducted in such a manner, that only one half of the whole number retire each year. (See Syn. Dord. Art. 27) But this does not forbid the liberty of immediately choosing the same persons again, if from any circumstances it may be judged expedient to continue them in office, by a reelection.

This article simply expands on Rule 27 of Dort.

ART. XXIX.

When matters of peculiar importance occur, particularly in calling a minister, building of churches, or whatever relates immediately to the peace and welfare of the whole congregation, it is usual (and it is strongly recommended upon such occasions, always) for the consistory to call together all those who have ever served as elders or deacons, that by their advice and counsel they may assist the members of the consistory. These, when assembled, constitute what is called the *great Consistory*. From the object, or design of their assembling, the respective powers of each are easily ascertained; Those who are out of office, have only an advisory or counselling voice; and as they are not actual members of the board or corporation, cannot have a decisive vote. After obtaining the advice, it rests with the members of the consistory to follow the counsel given them, or not, as they shall judge proper. But unless very urgent reasons should appear to the contrary, it will be prudent and expedient in all cases, to comply with the advice of those, who from their numbers and influence in the congregation, may be supposed to speak the language of the people, and to know what will be most for edification and peace.

This article introduces a distinctive feature of the Reformed Church in America, the *Great Consistory*. The root of the feature is perhaps Rule 10 of Dort, which requires a departing pastor also to consult with the whole body of those in a congregation who have served as elder or deacon. But this article goes much further, recognizes this group of members with a specific title, and gives more occasions for them to be consulted, such as the calling of a new pastor. If this body, which still exists in the Reformed church, were to be employed as the article suggests, the Great Consistory would handle much of the business that is done in modern congregational meetings. Indeed, according to these articles, the only reason for the congregation ever to meet would be to elect elders and deacons, and if the third method were followed, as recommended, the congregation might never meet. Here the Reformed church starkly contrasts with Puritan and New England Congregationalism.

ART. XXX.

An office, the object of which solely respects keeping in repair the churches, the parsonage, and school-houses, and executing the orders which the consistory, from time to time, may make in regard to them, has, in most congregations, been appointed by the title of *Church-Masters*. These are annually elected by the Consistory, and may be continued where it has been customary, and is approved: for the consistory may appoint two or more of their own body, as a standing committee for that purpose, at their own discretion, and as they shall find to be most convenient.

Church masters were not mentioned in the Rules of Dort, but the office had arisen in North America, especially in the larger churches. This article simply recognizes the office without requiring it. The office later became much less common, and it is never mentioned in the Constitution of 1833 or thereafter.[10]

II,

OF

ECCLESIASTICAL ASSEMBLIES.

ART. XXXI.

All *ECCLESIASTICAL ASSEMBLIES* possess a right to judge and determine upon matters within their respective jurisdictions, and which are regularly, and in an ecclesiastical manner, brought before them. As every individual, who judges himself aggrieved, has a right of appealing from the decision of a lower assembly to an higher; so it is permitted to lower assemblies, when difficult or important cases are brought before them, to postpone a final determination, until they have laid the whole before an higher assembly. In all such references from a lower assembly to an higher, the latter may remit the case, with proper advice, back to the former, to be there decided; or, if it shall appear to be very important, and what may affect in its consequences, the general welfare of the churches, the higher assembly may take the case under its own immediate cognizance, and proceed in the same, either *de novo*, or upon the evidence produced in the records of the lower assembly.

This article modifies Rules 30 and 31 of Dort, and softens the boundaries between the higher and lower assemblies. A lower assembly may bring business to a higher one without there being a formal appeal, and in such case a higher assembly, in contradiction to Rule 30, may presume to take "under its own immediate cognizance" business that arguably could have remained in a lower one.

I.

Of CONSISTORIES.

ARTICLE XXXII.

The particular spiritual government of the congregation is committed to the consistory. It is therefore their duty at all times to be vigilant, to preserve discipline, and to promote the peace and spiritual interest of the congregation. Particularly, before the celebration of the Lord's Supper, a faithful and solemn inquiry is to be made, by the president of the consistory; whether to the knowledge of those present, any member in full communion had departed from the faith, or in walk or conversation has behaved unworthy the Christian profession? that such as are guilty may be properly rebuked, admonished, or suspended from the privilege of approaching the Lord's Table, and all offences may be removed out of the Church of Christ.

This and the following four articles expand Rule 37 of Dort. Article XXXIV makes it clear that while the classis *installs* pastors, it is the local consistories that have the sole right to select and call them.

ART. XXXIII.

Every consistory shall keep a record of its own acts and proceedings. And in every congregation a distinct and fair register shall be preserved by the minister, of every baptism and marriage there celebrated, and of all who are received as members in full communion.

ART. XXXIV.

Consistories possess the right of calling ministers for their own congregations. But in exercising this right they are bound to use their utmost endeavours, either by consulting with the great consistory, or with the congregation at large, to know what person would be most acceptable to the people.

ART. XXXV.

A neighbouring minister (if there is none belonging to the consistory) must be invited to superintent the proceedings, whenever a consistory is desirous of making a call. The instrument is to be signed by all the members of the consistory, or by the president, in the name of the consistory; and if the church is incorporated, it is proper to affix the seal of the corporation. When the call is completed, it must be laid by the consistory before the classis, and be approved by the same, before it can be presented to the person called.* And if the call be accepted, the approbation of the people must be formally obtained by the consistory (agreeably to art. iv. of the Church Orders,) before the minister may be ordained.

* In the United States of America, where civil and religious liberty are fully enjoyed, and where no ecclesiastical establishments can be formed by civil authority; the approbation of magistrates in the calling of Ministers, is not required or permitted. It was therefore judged proper in the translation of the Church orders to omit every paragraph which referred to any power of the magistrate, in ecclesiastical affairs, as a matter merely local and peculiar to the European establishments.

This article regulates the classis' supervision of a consistory which is proceeding to a call, by means of a neighboring pastor. This was not required in the Netherlands, where most consistories were on the collegiate style (one consistory for the whole city, with a number of congregations, and a number of pastors preaching in rotation), so that one of the consistory's own ministers could sign the call. The "approbation of the people" is not a congregational meeting, but the opportunity for anyone to raise an objection after the public reading of the call over three Sundays. The footnote to the article explains why the mention of the magistrate has been excised from Rule 37 of Dort.

ART. XXXVI.

The forms have hitherto varied. In many it has been customary to enumerate all the particular duties to be performed by the Minister: but as those duties are sufficiently ascertained, it is judged unnecessary to burthen the instrument with a repetition of what the very office of a Minister implies. For the sake of propriety therefore, as well as uniformity, it is recommended to the churches, for the future to adopt the following form of a call: viz.

To N. N.

Grace mercy and peace from GOD our FATHER, and JESUS CHRIST our LORD!

"WHEREAS the Church of Jesus Christ at ———, is at present destitute of the stated preaching of the word, and the regular administration of the ordinances, and is desirous of obtaining the means of grace, which God hath appointed for the salvation of sinners, through Jesus Christ his Son. AND WHEREAS the said Church is well satisfied of the piety, gifts and ministerial qualifications of you N. N. and hath good hope that your labours in the Gospel will be attended with a blessing. Therefore, we [*the stile and title of the said Church,*] have resolved to call, and hereby solemnly, and in the fear of the Lord, do call you the said N. N. to be our pastor and teacher, to preach the word in truth and faithfulness, to administer the holy sacraments agreeably to the institution of Christ, to maintain Christian discipline, to edify the congregation, and especially the youth by catechetical instructions, and, as a faithful servant of Jesus Christ, to fulfil the whole work of the Gospel Ministry, agreeably to the word of God, and the excellent rules and constitution of our reformed Dutch Church, established in the last national Synod held at Dordrecht, and ratified and explained by the ecclesiastical judicatory, under which we stand, and to which you, upon accepting this call, must with us remain subordinate.

"In fulfilling the ordinary duties of your Ministry, it is expressly stipulated, that besides preaching upon such texts of scripture, as you may judge proper to select for our instruction, you also explain a portion of the Heidelbergh Catechism on the Lord's days, agreeably to the established order of the reformed Dutch Church, and that you farther conform in rendering all that public service, which is usual, and has been in constant practice in our congregation; the particular service which will be required of you, is [*here insert a detail of such particulars, if any there be, which the situation of the congregation may render necessary; especially in case of combinations, when the service required in the respective congregations, must be ascertained; or when the Dutch and English languages are both requisite, the proportion of each may be mentioned, or left discretionary as may be judged proper.*]

"To encourage you in the discharge of the duties of your important office; we promise you in the name of this Church, all proper attention, love and obedience in the Lord; and to free you from worldly cares and avocations, while you are dispensing spiritual blessings to us, we the [*Elders and Deacons, &c. the stile and title of the Church.*] do promise and oblige ourselves to pay to you the sum of —, in — payments, yearly and every year as long as you continue the minister of this Church, together with [*such particulars as may refer to a parsonage or other emoluments.*] for the performance of all which, we hereby bind ourselves, and our successors firmly by these presents. The Lord incline your heart to a cheerful acceptance of this call, and send you to us in the fulness of the blessing of the Gospel of peace! done in consistory, and subscribed with our names this — day of — in the year —."

Attested by N. N. Moderator of the call.

Neither the Church Order nor the Post-Acta mandated the Form of a Call. The synod of 1790 produced a Form of the Call, and this was incorporated into the Explanatory Articles. Corwin asserts that Eilardus Westerlo was the Call's author.[11] It has evolved into the present "Call to a Minister" in the Formularies.

ART. XXXVII.

Consistories which have hitherto combined with one or more neighbouring consistories, in making calls and having a Minister to serve in common, may not at pleasure break such combination; but whenever their situation and circumstances render them capable of severally calling a Minister, a representation thereof must be made to the classis, and leave be first requested and obtained, before their former connections can be dissolved.

II.

CLASSIS

ART. XXXVIII.

The reformed Dutch Church holds the middle station, between two extremes. On the one hand, she denies all superiority of one Minister of Christ over another, and on the other, considers independent, unconnected congregations as unsafe and inconvenient. In order therefore, to unite both council and energy for the promotion of the spiritual interests of the Church, consistent with the liberty and dignity of the Gospel dispensation; her government is administered by classes, and Synods. A classis consists (Art. 41. Church orders) of all the Ministers, with each an Elder, and one Elder from every vacant congregation within a particular district. In this assembly, an immediate representation of all the Churches within those limits is formed; and a power of regulating the common measures for promoting religion, preventing error, and preserving peace within such district is lodged. To constitute a classis are required at least three ministers, and three Elders.

This article and the following six expand on Rule 41 of Dort. This article, like XVIII above, reveals that the North American church had to define itself against larger competitors which did not trouble the church in the Netherlands, Episcopalianism on one side and Congregationalism on the other.

ART. XXXIX.

Classes are invested with the power of approving or disapproving calls, and of ordaining or deposing Ministers, or dismissing them when called elsewhere. They have cognizance of whatever respects the welfare of their particular Churches, for the management of which the consistories may be incompetent. To the classes also appertain, the receiving and determining all appeals from consistorial adjudications; as well as all cases, respecting either Ministers or people which may arise within their jurisdiction, and are regularly brought before them. The forming new congregations, and determining the boundaries, when contested between congregations already formed; the continuing combinations, or the dissolution or change of the same, as may be requested by the people, or be judged necessary among the respective congregations.

Among the proper powers of classes, that of examining Students of Theology for their becoming candidates for the Ministry, and of candidates, for their becoming Ministers, is very important; and must always be attended to with great prudence, zeal, and fidelity. This power (which for certain reasons,) has hitherto been exercised only by the Synod, shall, agreeably to the government and discipline of the church, for the future, be also exercised by the respective classes.

This article gives more power to the classes than do the Dort rules themselves. First, "They have cognizance of whatever respects the welfare of their particular churches, for the management of which the Consistories may be incompetent." Second, the classes are given most of the responsibility for supervising theological students and candidates. This article is at the root of the development which distinguishes the Reformed Church in America from other Dutch Reformed groups, that the classis has evolved into the most powerful assembly within the structure.

ART. XL.

It shall be left to the discretion of every Student in Theology, to apply either to the Synod or to any classis he may choose for examination. But a candidate who has received a call, must be examined by the classis under whose jurisdiction the Church that has made the call is placed; unless such candidate should prefer being examined by the Synod.

ART. XLI.

At every examination of a Student or candidate by a classis, two of the Deputati Synodi shall be present, who shall see that the examination is performed with strictness, propriety and justice. That the Deputati may obtain proper and timely notice, it shall be the duty of the President of the last preceding classis, upon application being made to him for an examination, to send immediate information to the Deputati, and communicate the time and place when and where the same is to be held, in such manner that the Deputati shall be notified at least two weeks before such examination.

ART. XLII.

Every Classis shall keep a book, in which the forms of subscriptions for candidates and Ministers of the Gospel are fairly written, which those who are examined and approved, shall respectively subscribe in the presence of the classis. It shall also be the duty of every classis, annually to report to the Synod, all persons who have been examined and licensed, as well as those who have been ordained; and also, all removals of Ministers from one place to another, or by death, which may have happened within the jurisdiction of such classis, since the last session of Synod.

ART. XLIII.

Whenever the examination of a candidate for the Ministry, the approbation of a call, or any other *ordinary business* which could not be transacted at the stated meeting, shall render an extraordinary meeting of the classis necessary, it shall be the duty of the President of the last classis, upon application being made to him for that purpose, to call by circular letters the members together. And, whenever two Ministers and two elders belonging to the classis shall, upon *any occasion*, request in writing, under their hands, an extraordinary meeting, the president of the last classis may not refuse calling the same; provided that the expenses attending all extraordinary meetings of the classis shall be always supported by the persons or congregation, at whose request or for whose benefit such session is held.

ART. XLIV.

Once every year the Classis shall direct what shall be deemed necessary and practicable with regard to the visitation of the Churches, within their respective jurisdictions, and report the same to the Synod. For the more uniform and proper execution of this important duty, such particular questions and inquiries as shall be agreed upon, in any general Synod for that purpose, shall be inserted in the book of records of every classis, and by the visitors be faithfully proposed to the Minister, elders, and the deacons of every congregation in their respective visitations.

This article regulates Rules 41 and 44 of Dort.

III.

PARTICULAR SYNODS

ART. XLV.

A PARTICULAR SYNOD consists of a delegation of two Ministers, and two elders from a number of classes, (Church orders, Art. 47.) and constitutes a representation of all the particular Churches within those respective Classes.

This article and the following expand on Rule 47 of Dort. This article increases the power of a particular synod, however, by giving it "original cognizance of such cases are not merely local," apparently at its own discretion.

ART. XLVI.

Synods have power to receive and determine all appeals and references properly brought from the classes; and to take original cognizance of such cases as are not merely local, and which in their consequences are supposed to affect the general welfare of the Church.

ART. XLVII.

Notwithstanding the power of examination is conferred upon the classes, the particular Synods, (until it be otherwise determined in the general Synod) will continue as heretofore, to examine and license; and it shall still remain in the choice of any Student in Theology, or of any candidate who has received a call to be examined by the Synod: but with this express declaration, that the examinations held by any classis, and the certificate given by the president of a classis, shall be considered as equally proper, authentic and valid, as those done and conferred by a Synod.

This article and the two following expand on Rule 49 of Dort. In spite of the classis taking chief responsibility for the examination and licensure of students, the right is reserved for a student to seek this from a particular synod.

ART. XLVIII.

A copy of the minutes of every session of the classis, held since the last session of Synod, shall, at the opening of the Synod, be produced and laid upon the table for the inspection of the members. The reports of each classis respecting the candidates, Ministers, ordinations, and removals made within their jurisdictions, shall not only be mentioned in the minutes of the Synod, but be regularly inserted by the scriba of the Synod, in a register preserved for that purpose by the Synod.

ART. XLIX.

When any particular business cannot be finished at the annual session of Synod, or when any matter is foreseen to claim their attention, which ought to be dispatched before the next usual time of meeting, it shall be in the power of Synod to adjourn to any future day, and hold an extraordinary session. Whenever also two of the Deputati Synodi, shall represent to the president of the last Synod, the necessity of calling an extraordinary Synod, and shall in writing request him so to do, it shall be the duty of such president by circular letters to the members of the last Synod, to summon an extra session, for the express purpose suggested by the Deputati; which business, and no other whatever, shall then be transacted.

ART. L.

The particular Synods shall continue to exchange every year a copy of their Acts with the Synod of North-Holland, and express in their letters the desire of the reformed Church in America, to preserve a connection and cultivate a correspondence, which they highly esteem and have found to be beneficial.

This article is an application of Rule 48 of Dort, the North American Particular Synod now being parallel to the Synod of North Holland. The required correspondence did not last long. At the synod of 1800, a committee reported that "no answers have been received to the letters written for several years to the Synod of North Holland, probably owing to the interrupted state of affairs in that country," referring to the Napoleonic Wars. The exchange of Acts was never regularly maintained. The North American Synod had become a completely independent church.

IV.

GENERAL SYNOD

ART. LI.

A General Synod represents the whole body. It is the highest judicatory, and the last resort in all questions, which relate to the government, peace, and unity of the Church. To this is committed the superintending the interests of religion, the maintaining harmony, and faithfully preserving the Churches in the principles and practice of their holy religion.

This and the following four articles expand on Rule 50 of Dort.

ART. LII.

To the general Synod alone shall appertain the power of nominating and appointing professors of Theology; of constituting them emeriti, and declaring their places vacant; of calling them to account for their doctrines or conduct, and when found guilty, of punishing them by admonition, suspension or total removal, as the case may require.

To the general Synod is referred the right of corresponding with other Churches; and particularly of superintending and preserving the correspondence which has long been maintained between the reformed Church in the Netherlands and this Church. For which purpose a copy of the Letters sent by the particular Synod, and those received by them with the state of the correspondence since the last recess of every general Synod, shall be reported by the particular Synod, at every ordinary session of the general Synod.

To the general Synod belongs the receiving and issuing all appeals from particular Synods; and proceeding and determining all references which are regularly brought, agreeably to such regulations and restrictions, as shall for that purpose be made and determined.

Finally, to the general Synod belongs the forming of new particular Synods, and properly organizing the same; the ascertaining their boundaries, and judging and determining all disputes that may arise at any time, respecting such boundaries.

The article restates the establishment of the professorate as the right of the General Synod alone. Correspondence with other denominations is reserved for the General Synod. The reason that this included the review of the correspondence with the Synod of North Holland (at the particular synod level) was that there was no general synod in the Netherlands. The right to organize new particular synods belonged to the civil government in the Netherlands, here it is given to the General Synod. But no other new original powers are granted to it.

ART. LIII.

As the holding a general Synod (agreeably to Art. 50. of the Church Orders) has been found to be inconvenient in the Netherlands, and the Churches there have adopted a mutual correspondence from the particular Synods as a substitute; so the situation and particular circumstances of the reformed Dutch Church in America, render an alternative in the organization of a general Synod, equally necessary. It is, therefore, resolved that, instead of being composed of Delegates from the particular Synods, the general Synod shall continue as heretofore, to consist of all the Ministers, with each an Elder, and also, an Elder from every vacant congregation. This mode of constituting a general Synod shall remain, until some other substitute, or the obtaining a sufficient number of Delegates from particular Synods shall be found practicable, and by a formal resolution of the general Synod for the time being shall be regularly adopted. And all the powers and rights before recited are and shall continue to be vested in the general Synod organized agreeably to the present form.

This article differs from the Dort rules by organizing the General Synod, for the time being, as a convention, seating every pastor and an elder from every consistory. It returned to the original pattern of seating only delegates of the classes in 1812. In 1815 the General Synod began to meet annually.

ART. LIV.

The general Synod shall assemble once every three years, on such days, either in the months of May or June, and at such place as shall, at every preceding ordinary general Synod be determined. Any ten ministers, and ten elders or more, from a majority of the several classes being met on the day, and at the place appointed, shall be deemed sufficient to form a general

Synod and proceed upon business.

ART. LV.

The general Synod shall keep a regular and distinct record of all its proceedings; and may adjourn or make such regulations from time to time, for calling an extraordinary session as shall be judged convenient and necessary.

III.

OF

USAGES AND CUSTOMS

ART. LVI.

The zeal of the reformed Church, for initiating children early in the truth, [expressed, Art. 54th of the Church Orders, where care is taken that schoolmasters shall be of the reformed religion] cannot be evidenced in the same manner in America, where many denominations of Christians, and some who do not even profess the Christian religion, inhabit promiscuously; and where schoolmasters can seldom be found who are members of the church. In such a situation, it is recommended to parents to be peculiarly attentive to the religious education of their children, not only by instructing them, and daily praying with them at home, but by never employing schoolmasters whose characters are unascertained or suspicious, and especially none who scoff at the holy scriptures or whose conduct is immoral.

It is also further recommended, that parents endeavour to prevail upon schoolmasters to make the children belonging to the Dutch church, commit to memory, and publicly repeat in the school, one section of the Heidelbergh Catechism, at least once every week.

This article responds to Rules 53 and 54 of Dort. With the Reformed church being disestablished, it could no longer control the common schools; at the same time, it presumed a generally Protestant culture. To satisfy Rule 54, a Form of Subscription for Schoolmasters was drafted at Dort (Post-Acta, Session 165), but the form is passed over, since it was now hardly enforceable.

ART. LVII.

As a register must be kept by every minister of all the baptisms celebrated in his church, [see Exp. Art. 33.] it is necessary for all who desire to have their children baptised, previously to apply to their minister for that purpose. Such applications also afford an opportunity to the Minister of explaining the nature of the ordinance of baptism, and pressing upon the conscience of the parent, the duties incumbent upon him as a professing Christian; and to which, in particular, by this holy sacrament, he is obliged. The custom which has prevailed in some congregations of applying to the clerk of the church, for registering infants who are to be baptised, shall be abolished, and for the future, none but ministers shall perform that service.

This article and the following three interpret Rules 56 through 60 of Dort. They attempt to maintain a generally high baptismal discipline, expecting the pastor to educate and admonish the baptizing parents, emphasizing the use of the liturgical form at a public worship service, and giving the consistory some measure of responsibility. Special circumstances are provided for, but carefully disciplined.

ART. LVIII.

The sacrament of baptism ought always to be administered in the church, at the time of public worship, [see Church Ord. Art. 56.] and the forms adopted for baptism, consider it as celebrated in public. Baptising in private families, is therefore to be discountenanced, and as much as possible avoided. In cases however, of the sickness of the parents and especially of the infant, it is lawful to administer this sacrament in private. In other cases which may have something singular in their circumstances, it is left to the conscientious discretion of the minister to comply with the requests of parents for private baptism or not, as he shall judge proper. In this however, he is to consider himself responsible to his consistory, if questioned thereon. But no private baptism shall be administered without the presence of at least one elder, who shall accompany the minister for that purpose, and the same form and solemnity shall be always used as in public baptism.

ART. LIX.

In the church there is no difference between bond and free, but all are one in Christ. Whenever therefore, slaves or black people shall be baptised or become members in full communion of the church, they shall be admitted to equal privileges with all other members of the same standing, and their infant children shall be entitled to baptism, and in every respect be treated with the same attention that the children of white or free parents are in the church. Any minister, who upon any pretence, shall refuse to admit slaves or their children, to the privileges to which they are entitled, shall, upon complaint being exhibited and proved, be severely reprimanded by the Classis to which he belongs.

This article is a notable benchmark. Such phrases as "equal privileges," "the same standing," and "treated with the same atten-

tion," served to help the North American branch of the Dutch
Reformed church avoid the course that the South African branch
would later follow, lacking, as it did, this article. The actual
practice of the Reformed church, however, was not up to the
standard of the article, and not until 1819, for example, were
"colored people" included in membership statistics.[12] Many congregations continued to seat "colored" members in the rear portions of their galleries until well into the nineteenth century.

ART. LX.

With respect to godfathers and godmothers, or witnesses, as
they are called, [see Art. 57, Church Ord.] the meaning of the
Reformed Church is sufficiently explained in the Synod, held at
Wisel, in the year 1568, Chap. I, Art. 10. "We hold it among
matters which are to be accounted indifferent whether any
witnesses are taken in baptism, or whether to the parents alone,
together with the whole congregation, the charge of baptised
children is committed." And again, Chap. VI, Art. 3. "The custom
of having particular witnesses who are called godfathers and
godmothers, is left to be followed or not, as each one shall
choose."

ART. LXI.

Great attention shall always be paid by all the ministers of the
gospel to the instruction of youth and others, in their respective
congregations, in order to prepare them to make a confession of
their faith, and from proper principles and right views, as
members in full communion, to approach the Lord's table. If any
Minister shall habitually neglect to catechise the children and
youth of his congregation, it shall be the duty of the elders to urge
him to it; and if he shall without a sufficient reason,
notwithstanding the remonstrance of his elders, continue to
neglect the same for one whole year; he shall be reported by his

elders to the classis, that measures may be taken to oblige him to fulfil, what the reformed Dutch Church has always considered, a very important and necessary part of the ministerial duty.

This article and the following two regulate Rules 61 and 62 of Dort. They serve to maintain a generally high Communion discipline. Even though the Table is to have a "fence" around it, the pastor is responsible to instill, through catechism, a proper appreciation for Communion, especially among the young.

ART. LXII.

None can be received as members in full communion, or be suffered to partake at the Lord's table, unless they first shall have made a confession of their faith, or have produced a certificate of their being members in full communion of some reformed Church. All such shall be reported by the minister to the consistory, and be approved by them, and published to the congregation, before they can be registered as regular members in the Church. Members, who are known to be such from other congregations, may be admitted to occasional communion, upon application to the minister.

ART. LXIII.

In Article 23, of the Church orders, it is mentioned as a duty incumbent upon ministers and elders, to visit the members in full communion of their respective congregations, previous to the administration of the Lord's supper. These visitations, when performed with prudence and proper solemnity, have been found to be productive of many good and happy consequences. It is therefore expected that every minister, accompanied with an elder, will (unless it be judged impracticable by the consistory) at least once in every year, visit all the members of his Church, and endeavor to remove all animosities that may have arisen, and excite them to peace and proper exercises of faith and holiness. Ministers and elders who shall habitually neglect this duty, shall be called to account in their respective classes, and be prompted to attend to the same. And all classes are enjoined to make particular inquiry whether this duty is punctually fulfilled in the respective congregations within their district.

In connection with Communion, this article recapitulates Rule 23 of Dort and the practice of "House Visitation" (*huisbezoek*). The article specifically makes classis responsible to see that the consistory does it.

ART. LXIV.

If any member of the reformed Dutch Church shall choose to submit any book or writing on religious subjects, previous to its publication, to the approbation of Synod, and makes application for that purpose; the Synod may appoint the professors of Theology, or any number of their members as a special committee for revising such book or writing, and approving and recommending the same, if it shall be deemed proper. The 55th Article of the Church orders is to be no further extended, nor is it in any other mode practised upon by the reformed Dutch Church in America.

This article limits Rule 55 of Dort. The scope is narrowed to "religious subjects," and it is made wholly voluntary.

ART. LXV.

No Psalms or Hymns may be publickly sung in the reformed Dutch Churches, but such as are approved and recommended by the general Synod. [Church Ord. Art. 69.] In the reformed Dutch Church in America, the following are approved and recommended, viz.

In the Dutch language, the version of Dathenus, and the new version of Psalms and Hymns, compiled and adopted in the Netherlands, in the year 1773. In the English language the Psalms and Hymns compiled by professor Livingston, and published with the express approbation and recommendation of the General Synod, in the year 1789. In the French language, the Psalms and Hymns compiled by Theodore De Beza and La Moret. And in the German language the Psalms and Hymns, published at Marburgh and Amsterdam, and now used in the reformed Churches in Germany, in the Netherlands, and in Pennsylvania.

This article interprets Rule 69 of Dort. Four different psalters are considered to satisfy the rule. A fifth one, the New-York *Psalms of David* (1767), is ignored.[13]

ART. LXVI.

The Church of Christ is the best discerner of the times, and of the duties, to which the providence of God may call his people. The Church ought therefore, when it is judged proper, not only to request the civil rulers to set apart days of fasting and prayer or thanksgiving; but it may in its respective judicatories, call the people to those duties, either within the limits of a congregation, a classis, or a Synod.

This article expands Rule 66 of Dort. Not only can the Church petition the Government to call "days of public fasting and prayer," it may schedule its own, apart from the public.

ART. LXVII.

That the reformed Church does not believe the days usually called holy days are of divine institution, or by preaching on those

days [see Art. 67 of Church Orders] intends any thing more than
to prevent evil, and promote the edification of the people, is
evident from the contents of the 53d Art. of the Synod of
Dordrecht held in the year 1574. "With regard to feast days, upon
which besides the Lord's day, it has been customary to abstain
from labour, and to assemble in the Church, it is resolved that we
must be contented with the Lord's day alone. The usual subjects
however of the birth of Christ, of his resurrection, and sending of
the holy spirit, may be handled and the people be admonished,
that these feast-days are abolished." In the national Synod held
at Middleburgh, in Zealand, in the year 1581, Art. 50, it is said "In
places where the feast days are celebrated, the ministers shall
endeavour, by preaching at such times, to change the
unnecessary and hurtful idleness of the people into holy and
edifying exercise."

This article interprets Rule 67 of Dort in a somewhat Puritan
direction. It cites the Provinical Synod of Dordrecht in 1574,
which attempted to do away with holidays altogether, and the
Middleburgh Synod of 1581, which, though a little more tolerant,
still discouraged them. But these were the two synods most
strongly influenced by English Calvinism, with its repudiation of
the "calendar." By the time of the National Synod of Dort,
however, the Dutch church had taken a more moderate and even
positive attitude toward the "holy-days." English and Scottish
pastors serving in the Netherlands were later brought up on
charges for not observing them.[14] Does this article show a
renewed influence by English and Scottish Calvinism?

ART. LXVIII.

In consequence of abuses which have frequently arisen from the
practice of preaching funeral sermons, the 65th Article of the
Church Orders is strictly adhered to; but as it is often found to
answer a good purpose, to speak a word of exhortation at the
time of funerals, the right of addressing the people upon such

occasions, is left to be exercised by every minister at his own discretion.

This article softens the prohibition in Rule 65 of Dort.

IV.

DISCIPLINE

ART. LXIX.

No accusation or process is admissible before an ecclesiastical judicatory but when offences are alleged which, agreeably to the word of God, deserve the censure of the church. Nor shall any complaint of a private nature be noticed, unless the rules prescribed by the Lord Jesus, Matt. xviii, have been strictly followed. Neither shall complaint in cases of scandal be admitted, unless such complaints are brought forward within the space of one year and four months after the crime shall be alleged to have been committed; excepting, when it shall appear that unavoidable impediments prevented the bringing an accusation sooner.

This article and the following apply to Rules 71 through 74 of Dort. This article reinforces the requirement that the Matthew 18 procedure be followed. It introduces a "statute of limitations" of sixteen months. The following article reinforces the requirement in Rule 74 of two witnesses and strictly disciplines the course of any trial for the protection of all involved.

ART. LXX.

To establish an accusation against any member of the church, the testimony of more than one witness is required. Their witness shall be given under a solemn declaration upon the faith and credibility of a Christian, or of an oath taken before a magistrate, at the discretion of the judicature. Every trial, in all judicatories, from the highest to the lowest, shall be deliberate and impartial. The sum of the evidence shall be faithfully minuted. The sentence shall always be entered at large on the records. And all the parties shall immediately be allowed copies of the testimony and sentence, and of the whole proceedings, if they demand the same.

ART. LXXI.

Ministers of the gospel must be an example to believers, and much of their success will usually depend upon their good character, and their holy walk and conversation. Their conduct must therefore be watched over with great attention, and their crimes punished with impartiality and severity. In admitting accusations against a minister, the rule prescribed by the Apostle, 1 Tim. v. 19, shall always be observed; and accusers must come forward openly to support the charge, unless where common fame has rendered a scandal so notorious, that the honour of religion shall require an investigation.

This article and the following expand on Rules 79, 80, and 81 of Dort. This article admonishes pastors to be above reproach, but also limits the right of others to accuse them. First Timothy 5:19 states, "Against an elder receive not an accusation, but before two or three witnesses" (KJV). The term *elders*, in this chapter, was held to apply to both pastors and elders (as in *The Form for ordaining Elders and Deacons* in the Liturgy).[15]

ART. LXXII.

When it is said (Art. 79 of the Church Orders) that ministers guilty of atrocious crimes shall be suspended from the exercise of their office by the consistory, until they are tried by the classis, it is only intended, that in certain public and notorious offences, which would render the appearance of a minister in the pulpit in such a situation, highly offensive; it shall be the duty of the consistory, in order to prevent scandal, to shut the door against such criminal, and refer him to be tried by the classis, as soon as possible. The proceedings of the consistory in such cases, is at their peril, and is not to be considered as a trial, but only a prudent interference, and binding over the person accused, to the judgment of his peers.

This article interprets Rule 79 of Dort. Consistories are responsible for their ministers, yet their ministers are not amenable to them. They are specifically given the right, at their discretion, to "shut the door," or close the pulpit to their pastor, but "at their peril," and once such a course of action is taken it must then immediately be referred to the classis, the body to which the minister is solely amenable.

ART. LXXXIII.

The forms and proceedings in the respective judicatories shall always be, as far as possible, agreeable to established precedents and usages. In cases which appear to be new and difficult it is recommended to the lower judicatories to refer their difficulties to the higher, for direction; and to the higher, as well as to the lower to proceed with peculiar deliberation, and always agreeable to the word of God, and the ordinances and constitution of the reformed Dutch Church.

Respecting these explanatory articles, the general Synod declare that they contain the principal out-lines of the practice of their church; agreeably to which the ecclesiastical ordinances of the national Synod, held at Dordrecht, in the years, 1618, and 1619, and which were solemnly and formally recognised and adopted, at the convention, held at New-York, in the year 1771, are proceeded upon, and executed. And the general Synod further declare, that these articles are to be considered as subjected to such additional explanations and alterations as shall be found necessary to throw light upon any article of the church orders of the Synod of Dordrecht aforesaid, or be judged proper to remove any doubts or difficulties. With this express provision, however, that no alterations, or explanations shall ever be made, but by previous recommendations from the general Synod to the respective classes, and the consent of a majority of the same to such proposed alterations, or explanations, together with the final determination and resolution of the general Synod for the time being.

The preceding Explanatory Articles were ratified in the General Synod, held at New-York, the 10th day of October, 1792, and were Signed,

SOLOMON FRÆLIGH, Præses,
JOHN BASSETT, Scriba,
PETER STRIKER, Scriba.

This declaration establishes the system of constitutional change and amendment which still holds in the Reformed church. Unlike other Dutch Reformed denominations (such as the Christian Reformed church) the General Synod may not itself alter the Church Order, or any other part of the Constitution, without the changes first receiving the endorsement of a majority of the several classes, and then receiving the approval of a second General Synod. (Since 1916 any amendment requires the approval of two-thirds of the classes.) The long term effect of this amendment process has been to strengthen the power of the classes at the expense of the synod, but also to strengthen the "constitutional" character of the Reformed church.

VI

The History of the Constitution After 1793

Church and State

There was a double, almost contradictory, purpose for the 1793 constitution. Its first purpose was to *preserve* the tradition, to keep the North American Dutch church still firmly established upon the Netherlandic Constitution which was represented by the Synod of Dort. Its second purpose was to *cause change* in the tradition, to adapt the Dutch church to the new situation, and to let it unfetter itself from whatever shackles the tradition imposed on it. The 1792 synod appears to have believed that it accomplished both these purposes, preservation and change.

As the previous chapters show, the two shackles the church was most happy to be free of were, first, the old European church-state connection, and, second, the old assumption of exclusivity. Getting rid of the first made the Dutch church a free church. Of course, even in the colonial era most of the congregations in the villages and countryside were functionally free churches. Only a few of the city congregations had royal charters. The church-state connection was dead in practice; the new constitution killed it in principle. Freeing itself of the second shackle, exclusivity, made the Dutch church an ecumenical church (to use a modern term anachronistically). It formally recognized the equal validity of other religious denominations and their right to exist within the same body politic. Judging by the preface to *The Constitution*, the leaders of the synod were quite intentional about the necessity of these changes, but they did not think these changes necessarily contradicted what they had also been trying to preserve.

Recently, however, two Reformed church scholars, Eugene Heideman and James Van Hoeven, have suggested that the 1792 synod, and Livingston especially, changed more than they thought, even to the extent of changing exactly what they thought they were preserving. These scholars have argued that a whole new doctrine of the church was brought in by the framers of *The Constitution*, a doctrine which was actually contradictory to the doctrine of the church according to Dort.[1] These scholars make a significant point, for while the preface states that the church is "a bond of union wholly voluntary," the Synod of Dort would never have said this. Heideman and Van Hoeven interpret such a statement to be "Livingston's adaptation of the American Puritan principle of voluntary church membership." They are undoubtedly correct in their judgment that viewing the church in this way would have enormous implications for such other Dutch Calvinist doctrines as election, atonement, and the nature of the sacraments, especially infant baptism.

Of course, in the middle colonies of North America, "voluntary church membership" was a fact of life for all denominations, no matter what their theology, and without regard for "Puritan principles." Even though a few of the city congregations had royal charters and enjoyed some of the privileges of establishment, the great majority of Dutch Reformed congregations were purely voluntary religious societies which people could join or leave at will, and did so. They were *de facto* "free churches." So the whole new doctrine of the church was already in operation long before the 1793 constitution, even if it was not officially acknowledged as such. If the framers of the constitution were responsible for any change in the doctrine of the church, it was simply to acknowledge theologically an existing reality.

Is it correct to say that John Henry Livingston imported "Puritan principles" into the Dutch church? We know that Livingston studied at Yale, where he might easily have absorbed such principles. We know that, later on, while Livingston was editor of all the Dutch Reformed liturgical books, he deleted a paragraph from the Baptism Liturgy, the so-called Flood Prayer which had originated with Martin Luther. The Flood Prayer evoked a corporate and mystical doctrine of the church in a manner that might have made an "American Puritan" uncomfortable. So it is not unreasonable to say that Livingston represents some sort of a change in the doctrine of the church.

But one must be careful in how one says this. First, one must speak carefully about the Puritans. Their principle of "voluntary church membership" was not necessarily antithetical to the principle of established churches. After all, it was the two Puritan states of Connecticut and Massachusetts which maintained the congregational churches as "established churches" well into the nineteenth century. When it comes to the Dutch, it must be pointed out that for a long time even the church in the Netherlands had been greatly influenced by Puritanism (though not of the American sort). Also, there were many other Dutch pastors, never having set foot in New England, who skipped over the Flood Prayer when they read the Baptism Liturgy. Finally, it is probably most accurate to accuse Livingston of importing, if anything, Presbyterianism into the Dutch church rather than Puritanism. Livingston, for example, did not oppose the use of creeds and liturgical forms. Still, something happened while Livingston was leader which made the North American Dutch church define itself very differently from the European Dutch church.

If Livingston and his colleagues caused a change in the doctrine of the church, it was certainly not intentional. If anything, they thought they were preserving the doctrine of the church and actually restoring it to its purer Reformation roots. They thought they were setting the church free from its entanglement with the state, an entanglement which had only compromised the church. This was the real point of their having called the church a "bond of union wholly voluntary." They were making a political statement, not a strictly theological one. The roots of that statement were probably sunk more deeply into the political philosophy of John Locke, as John Coakley has recently shown,[2] than in the theology of Puritanism. It was in a highly charged political atmosphere that *The Constitution* was drafted and its preface written, when the United States was debating its own constitution, when the Christian churches were considered more central to political life than they are now, and when the several denominations were trying to determine their rightful place within "the new constellation."

However, since politics has everything to do with theology, a political statement cannot help but have theological implications. It cannot be denied that a principle of voluntary church membership had, by this time, entered the Reformed church. What Livingston might have defended as a restoration of the church's independence from the State, Van Hoeven has called a "Puritan (and Anabaptist) adaptation." Whether it was Puritan, Anabaptist, Presbyterian, or Lockean, there it was. Maybe it was all four.

Perhaps we need to look for a deeper influence as well. One of the most significant differences between the world of Livingston and the world of the Synod of Dort was the change in the status of the individual. During the 150 years between Dort and Livingston, the individual had become the center of the world. Livingston could not have restored the Reformation doctrine of the church if he'd wanted to. In the 1570s, the Dutch War of Independence from Spain had secured the rights and liberties of certain cities, provinces, and civic corporations. By contrast, 200 years later, the American War of Independence had secured the rights and liberties of the individual. So although it may be true that Livingston nudged the doctrine of the church in a more Puritan direction, wasn't that only a consequence of a much more encompassing and inexorable movement in Western civilization? People themselves had changed, the Enlightenment was in between them and the Reformation. They were individuals. The United States was the first political entity to recognize and celebrate it. And the leadership of the Dutch Reformed church was those pastors that had supported the Revolution. Could the doctrine of the church have turned out any differently in such a situation?

There is no doubt that one significant result of the view that the church is a voluntary association of individuals was that the Reformed church surrendered its historic responsibilities in the arena of politics. As Heideman has written more recently:

> The Church Order of Dort assumed that the civil authorities are ordained of God to care for public welfare and justice in society. It assumed that the church may

speak to the public officials on the basis of the gospel rather than simply on the basis of some form of enlightened thought. Private faith and public life can and should be interconnected. While Dort insisted upon a clear distinction between church and state, it did not separate religion from public life.

The Explanatory Articles opened the door to the notion that preachers should confine their sermons to matters of personal faith and private morals. In 1792 it was not yet known that a great divorce between Christ and culture was imminent; it would take almost two centuries to make that apparent. Since 1792, however, the theological basis on which the church may speak to the great public issues of the day has not been clear. The RCA continues to hesitate between its heritage and its experience on matters of private faith and public life.[3]

Heideman is certainly correct. The "heritage" of the RCA includes Ulrich Zwingli and John Calvin. For both of them, the church had everything to do with public political issues. In the Netherlands this remained so, in principle at least, until after World War II, but there, too, individualism has now changed everything. Of course, in North America, the Dutch church was so much smaller than the other denominations that it is difficult to believe that its voice would have been noticed by any political entity, but it is probably true that the church was hesitant to raise it. The effect of what happened is beyond dispute, even if one might disagree *why* it happened. If we compare our own Reformed Church in America with its sister denominations in the Netherlands and even South Africa, we find in our church a much weaker sense of public witness and cultural responsibility.

Revisions of the Constitution

The combination of preservation and change that the framers of the constitution enshrined in its three-fold shape has been maintained to this day, although much within it has been revised over the years. The Rules of Government were revised five times, in 1833, 1874, 1916, 1959, and 1968.[4] The Doctrine has remained the same, except for new translations and the eventual deletion of the Compendium. The Liturgy has also kept its place in the constitution, although in 1906, 1968, and 1987 it was considerably revised and expanded. The process of revision is a relatively slow one, however, because even the slightest change in the liturgical text must be treated as a constitutional amendment.

The 1793 edition of *The Constitution* served the church for a whole generation. In 1815 it appeared in a new edition, to which was added, as an appendix, the Rules of Order of the General Synod (not a part of the constitution proper) and a number of important synodical resolutions. Another edition appeared in 1834, which included the newly revised Rules of Government of 1833, plus the Rules of Order of Synod and the Formularies. In spite of the title page mentioning the Doctrinal Standards and Liturgy, they were not included. They were restored in the 1840 edition. In 1868, at the request of Classis Holland, the whole constitution was published in a Dutch version for use among the new immigrant churches.[5]

Again in 1869 an edition of *The Constitution* was published which lacked the Standards and Liturgy, despite their being listed on the title page. However, besides the Rules of Government, Formularies, and Rules of Order of Synod, the edition included a Digest of General Synod Legislation. In 1876 an edition appeared which incorporated the 1874 revision of the Rules of Government, but also lacked the Standards and Liturgy. In 1877 the Dutch edition was republished, as well as a new German edition.[6] In 1879 an edition came out which included all three parts of *The Constitution*, Doctrine, Liturgy, and Government. This was the very last time this would be so. The edition of 1885 contained only the Rules of Government, the Formularies, and the Rules of Synod. In 1885, in response to an overture from the Classis of New Brunswick, the General Synod appointed a committee to prepare a critical edition of the whole constitution, including the Standards and the Liturgy. A preparatory report was given at the synod of 1886, but then nothing ever came of it, and no critical edition has ever appeared. After 1885 every edition of the published constitution would mention the Standards and Liturgy, but would not include them.

The constitution came to be equated, at least in practice, with only one part of it, the Rules of Government.[7]

The first revision of the Government was ratified by the General Synod of 1833. This revision incorporated a few of the amendments which had been adopted in the mean time, but, more important, combined into one document the eighty-six "Rules of the Church Order of Dort" with the seventy-three "Explanatory Articles." The resultant Rules of Government, 118 paragraphs, was on the same general plan as the Rules of Dort, although it was divided differently. In the Rules of Dort each paragraph was an Article, while in the new Rules of Government each paragraph was a "Section." The four chapters were now divided into sub-chapters, and each of these sub-chapters took the title, "Article." The numbering of sections and articles was not consecutive; each chapter began with its own Article I, and each article began with its own Section 1.

The Rules of 1833 introduced the practice that when a pastor left one church for another, a neighboring pastor was to supervise the consistory's "instrument of dismission" and to deliver the same to the classis (I.I.18). The Rules defined the responsibility of the classes to supervise the admittance of candidates and pastors from other denominations (I.I.20-24). There was a new requirement that only male members of the church could become elders and deacons, and that only males could elect elders and deacons when forming new churches (I.III.3). The rules concerning church-masters and schoolmasters for general education were dropped.

The requirement of regular catechism preaching was maintained. The catechism was normally to be covered annually, but the "four year" schedule was for the first time admitted, though as an outer limit (II.II.13). The so-called "Constitutional Questions" were introduced (II.III.8). The classes were required annually to solicit answers to these from each of the consistories and to forward the answers to the particular and general synods. The Rules of 1833, when compared to Explanatory Article 39, somewhat narrowed the prerogatives of the classes, emphasizing their appellate power over the churches rather than their original power (II.III.2). Rules were also incorporated which defined the sizes of the particular and general synods.

The chapter, "Customs and Usages," deleted most of the catechetical and liturgical rules present in the 1793 constitution, such as the regulation of god-parents, holy-days, and the equality of black people in baptism and Communion. The minimum frequency for Communion was reduced to two times a year from four (III.I.2). For the first time, however, an "order of worship" appeared in the Rules, although not in the Liturgy itself (III.I.4).[8] The chapter on discipline represented the most thorough rewriting. The processes, the rights of the accused, and the responsibilities of the judicatories were carefully spelled out.

The next revision of the Rules of Government was ratified in 1874. This version was in substantial continuity with 1833, although there were no more chapter divisions and the Articles were numbered consecutively. The prerogatives of the classes were broadened again to include "a general superintendence over the spiritual interests and concerns of the several churches" (VII.2). The biggest change was a reorganization of the regulations on appeals and complaints (XIV.1-13). The rules were dropped which required synodical deputies to attend the classes' examinations of students and candidates. The General Synod was given the authority "to institute and organize" "general agencies" for missionary work (IX.4).

The third general revision of the Rules of Government was begun in 1910 and finished in 1916. Both the articles and the sections were now numbered consecutively. This version introduced the statement, "The Scriptures of the Old and New Testaments are its only rule of faith and practice" (I.2) and altered the Form of Subscription to make loyalty to the scriptures prior to loyalty to the Standards (I.18). The four-year cycle of catechism preaching was made standard (I.25). The Board of Direction was defined in the article on the General Synod (IX.112-3). Article X, "Of Customs and Usages," was very short. The "order of worship" was no longer outlined, but the one which by this time had been inserted in the Liturgy (of 1906) was mandatory (X.120). The Articles on Discipline and Complaints and Appeals were expanded. The amendment procedure was changed to require the approval of two-thirds of the classes (XIV.181). Ministers were made *ipso facto* members of their local churches.

Over the years the Rules of Government came to be amended

almost annually. In 1918 the synod established a Permanent Committee on the Revision of the Constitution to handle the amendments.[9] In 1955 this committee proposed a general rearrangement of the Rules.[10] This resulted in the fourth major revision, which was finished in 1959. There was a new scheme of articles, under such new headings as "Churches" and "Deacons." Each article began with its own Section 1, and the sections were no longer numbered consecutively. The revision fine-tuned the relationship of the minister to the local church and to the classis (2.2). It provided a procedure for licensing the graduates of non-RCA seminaries (3.2.c). It recast the Formula of Subscription in order to end on a more positive note (3.15). (A year later the title "Formula" was changed to "Declaration."[11]) The revision defined all judicatories as "permanent and continuing bodies" (5.1). This was a significant step away from the very conservative interpretation of the Dutch tradition, which held that the higher assemblies ceased to exist between meetings. The revision, perhaps inadvertently and for the first time, defined elders as "laymen" (6.2a). It gave definitions for associate and assistant ministers (8.22-23), which represents another significant step away from Dort, with its strict emphasis on the absolute equality of ministers. It gave the classes "authority to exercise all ecclesiastical functions in harmony with this Constitution, not specifically delegated to other judicatories." This has come to be called the "reserve clause," since it reserves for the classes all functions not specifically given to the other levels of church government. This climaxed the general trend in the RCA, which had begun already in 1793, of strengthening the classes in relation to the synods and the consistories. The revision also gave the classes a procedure for receiving candidates and ministers from other denominations (10.14-15).

The Revision Committee had proposed another significant change—the establishment of an Executive Council for the General Synod. This was to be a powerful and active "policy-formulating body."[12] The proposal received the required approval of two-thirds of the classes, but the General Synod of 1959, upon the advice of the president, withheld the declarative resolution which was required to adopt it in order to allow for consideration of a more general restructuring of the denomination.[13] In 1961 the General Synod appointed an Executive Committee with a three-year term. In 1965 the constitution was amended to make the Executive Committee a permanent feature.

The adoption of a new general revision did not have the effect, if that was the desire, of stabilizing the Rules of Government. Immediately they began to be revised and amended. Already in 1961 one classis overtured the General Synod to begin preparing "a new Constitution adequate for our time and need."[14] This overture failed, but in 1965 the General Synod directed the Committee on Revision to look into a wholesale recasting of the constitution.[15]

The Revision Committee reported the next year, 1966, and proposed what the Reformed church has today: first, a basic restructuring of the Rules of Government under the four headings of "consistory, classis, particular synod, General Synod"; second, the separating out of the judicial matters into an independent section called the "Disciplinary Procedures"; and third, new and more accurate titles: "The Government of the Reformed Church in America, Disciplinary Procedures, and the Organization and Rules of Order of the General Synod." The committee was instructed by the synod to consider removing the Liturgy from the constitution. This was the same synod which received a preliminary report proposing the centralization of all the denominational boards into a general program agency, and which also received a plan of merger with the Presbyterian Church in the United States.[16]

At the General Synod of 1967, the most controversial issue was the plan of merger. Almost unnoticed, a major revision of the Liturgy was accepted and the publication of the *Liturgy and Psalms* was announced. The new structure for program was adopted, creating the General Program Council. The Committee for Revision of the Constitution reported that its general "reorganization and rewriting of the Constitution" was underway. It recommended against removing the Liturgy from the constitution.[17] A year later, in 1968, the "reorganization and rewrite" had received the approval of considerably more than two-thirds of the respective classes, and the resulting *Book of Church Order* became the new standard for church government in the Reformed church.[18] A year later the merger with the Presbyterian Church in the United States was defeated. The Reformed church settled down to a period of consolidation after a few years of critical changes.

But once again, if there were any who thought that the second revision of the Government within a decade would stabilize the constitution, they were quickly disappointed. New amendments and proposals for revision were called for immediately. Indeed, a situation had developed in which, in the words of preamble to the Government, "the amendment of the church's document of government is an almost annual process." As a consequence, the General Synod of 1970 decided that the *Book of Church Order* should be published in loose leaf form, with replacement sheets distributed from time to time.[19]

For many people, the *Book of Church Order* (known as the *BCO*) is the constitution, even though it doesn't contain the Standards and the Liturgy, and even though it does contain the Rules of Order for the General Synod, which are not constitutional. The Government is a far cry from the Rules of Dort, having gone through five major revisions, and being now constantly, sometimes too hastily, revised. The first version of the Government lasted forty years, the second served another forty, the third another forty, the fourth about fifty, and the fifth less than ten. The double purposes of preservation and change have continued to be at work, although during the last few decades, it would seem that change has had the upper hand.

Revisions of the Liturgy

There were no authorized changes in the Liturgy for most of a century, but it wasn't long before unofficial and unauthorized changes began to corrupt the text. In the edition of the Liturgy that was included in the 1814 *Psalms and Hymns* (the edition that was in the hands of the people), the Consolation of the Sick had been abridged beyond recognition, and the Flood Prayer had been deleted from the Baptism Form. The edition of the Liturgy that was included in the 1815 *Constitution* also lacked the Consolation, although the Flood Prayer was present. In 1833 an Order of Worship was added to the Rules of Government, but not to the Liturgy itself. By the 1840 edition, the Flood Prayer had disappeared from *The Constitution* altogether. The result was that from 1814 to this day, the original North American Liturgy has been known to the church in the form of an incorrect "received text," instead of the 1793 constitution's proper text.[20]

The Liturgy came to be used by other churches in various parts of the world. The first such case was the Dutch Reformed church in South Africa. In 1840 the American church began to correspond with this distant branch of the same communion.[21] In 1853 the South African synod reported to the American synod that it had reprinted two parts of the constitution, the Doctrine and Liturgy, for the use of its English-speaking churches.[22] The South African edition was simply the post-1814 received text, with all its corruptions.[23] The second occasion for the spread of the Liturgy was the work of Reformed church missionaries, who translated it into at least four other languages. In 1862 it was published in Tamil for the use of the Reformed mission congregations in South India.[24] It was published in Telugu in 1891.[25] It was translated and published in Japanese probably about the same time.[26] In 1907 the Liturgy was translated into German for the use of immigrant congregations in the United States.[27]

Beginning in 1848, calls for the revision of the Liturgy were repeatedly brought to the synod. Two serious efforts at revision were initiated by the synod, in the years 1853 to 1858 and from 1868 to 1878, but neither set of changes got the required approval of the majority of the classes, except for the new Marriage Form of 1876. A number of the proposed new forms (for acts of worship not previously covered in the Liturgy) were permitted to be printed as "specimens" alongside the Liturgy, accompanied by the Psalms arranged for responsive reading, and this appeared in 1882.[28] The precise status of the new forms came to be debated in the denomination, and in 1889 the synod declared that the new forms were indeed part of the Liturgy.[29]

In 1906 the Liturgy was wholly revised and reorganized. The most important changes were the addition of abridged forms for the sacraments. The originals of these, in their post-1814 versions, were kept in. The original forms for ordinations, however, were entirely replaced by their abridgements, with the resultant loss of some good material. There were provided Orders for Morning and Evening Worship on the Lord's Day, which look very much like Anglican Morning and Evening Prayer. There was a whole new collection of General Prayers. As of 1906, the Reformed church had completely replaced the original Dutch Reformed order for Sunday service, which had survived, though truncated, in the original Prayers Before and After the Sermon. There were a number of other changes as well.[30]

By 1932 the further revision of the Liturgy had become a matter of constant discussion in the church, but there were no successful changes until after the Second World War, when the church began to be influenced by the Liturgical Movement.[31] In 1950 the General Synod initiated a long process of thorough and well-informed revision, which culminated in 1968 with the publication of the *Liturgy and Psalter* as the constitutional Liturgy.[32] This book became the generally accepted common service book of the Reformed church, and, as planned, was purchased in quantity by the congregations for putting in their pew racks. The 1968 sacramental forms, especially the Order for the Lord's Supper, have supplanted the earlier forms in general use, although the pre-1968 forms for the sacraments and discipline have been preserved and are used occasionally.[33]

The *Liturgy and Psalter* was written in the idiom of the Revised Standard Version of the Bible, which used "thee" and "thou" to address God. Unfortunately, the book was published just when the tide had turned against the use of those pronouns, and, to many minds, it was already obsolete, especially its 150 pages of responsive readings from the Psalms and Canticles. Furthermore, the book's four-year lectionary could not compete with the new Protestant adaptations of the three-year Roman lectionary. Thus, already in 1974 the General Synod agreed to a revision of the Liturgy that would modernize the language.[34]

A number of liturgical forms were produced over the next decade. One by one, they were presented before successive General Synods and the several classes as constitutional amendments. In 1987 these were gathered into a publication called *Worship the Lord*, which, by its title and appearance, was obviously meant to accompany *Rejoice in the Lord*, the denomination's new hymnal of 1985. Officially, *Worship the Lord* was simply a modern-language supplement to the 1968 *Liturgy*

and Psalter, since all the new liturgical forms in it were added to
the constitutional Liturgy, without replacing any of the forms
already established. Functionally speaking, however, the new
book was actually a replacement for the *Liturgy and Psalter*, since
it included all those liturgical forms which would make it
serviceable in the pew rack. Furthermore, except for the Order of
Worship for the Lord's Day, all the forms represent wholesale
rewritings rather than revisions. Congregations using *Worship
the Lord* would worship substantially differently from those
using the *Liturgy and Psalter*. As of 1987, therefore, the Liturgy
of the Reformed church could no longer be the major means of
unifying the denomination. *Worship the Lord* also contained the
Directory for Worship, which the General Synod adopted in 1986
as a "constituent part of the RCA *Constitution*, equal in authority
to the *Liturgy* of the RCA."[35] It has not been made clear what this
authority means, however.

Some congregations have remained loyal to the 1968 *Liturgy
and Psalter*, however, and there were a number of requests for its
reprinting. In response, "the General Synod in 1989 ordered the
reprinting of the liturgical forms in the 1968 *Liturgy and Psalms*
[sic] and the 1987 *Worship the Lord*."[36] The denominational
Worship Commission stated that since "the creation and revision
of liturgical forms is a continuous task in this area of rapidly-
changing language norms and parish needs," it had decided "to
gather all the forms into a loose-leaf binder," so that "provisional
and newly-approved forms can be added to the full collection."
The result is the bright red loose-leaf entitled, *Liturgy and
Confessions*. The great virtue of this publication is that once again
two parts of the constitution are available in a single source. But if
a constitution is that which a body can't change without changing
itself, the existence of *Liturgy and Confessions* in loose-leaf
raises the question of whether the Liturgy, despite its legal
status, really is constitutional anymore.

VII
Three Legs:
Interpreting the Constitution

Three-Legged Triangle

Since its first publication in 1793, the constitution of the Reformed church has had three main parts, Doctrine, Liturgy, and Government. These three parts fit together like the three legs of an equilateral triangle:

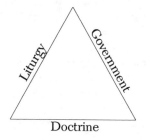

Doctrine is the basic leg of the triangle, upon which the other two legs rest. Doctrine is also called "dogma" or "belief." Doctrine is represented in the constitution by six documents, the three ecumenical creeds and the three Reformed confessions. The three Reformed confessions are also called the "Doctrinal Standards."[1] The two other legs of the triangle are the Liturgy, with all the Orders of Worship, and the Government, which is also called the Church Order, or "polity."[2]

In this triangle, all three legs are equal, all three are equally law for the church (not just the Government), all three are part of its confession (not just the Standards), and all three direct its worship (not just the Liturgy). For example, to define fully the office of pastor in the RCA, one must consult all three legs of the constitution. Likewise, to determine the whole meaning of Holy Baptism, one has to investigate all three legs. Or, to use a negative example, the act of excommunication involves both Government and Liturgy.

Each leg of this triangle supports the other two legs, and, in turn, each leg is supported by the other two. For example, there is a good deal of doctrine built into the Government, and there is even more doctrine built into the Liturgy. The doctrine in these other two legs not only strengthens them, it also reinforces the doctrine in the Confessions. Likewise, there is some polity included in the Confessions and in the Liturgy, and there is some worship in the Confessions and in the Government. It is very true of the constitution that "you can't tug at a finger of liturgy without immediately getting the whole hand of theology," and the same holds true for polity as well.[3]

The triangle is the strongest geometrical structure. The three legs make the constitution strong and steady, each leg reinforcing the other two. To weaken one is to weaken all three. It was after several years of careful work that the synod of 1791 settled on the three-legged shape of the constitution, looking hard at the old "Netherlandish Constitution" and finding the best way to adapt it to the whole new context of the United States of America. Their product has proven both stable and workable. One suspects that the threefold constitution has helped protect the RCA from many outside temptations, as well as from some of its own weaknesses.

Prophet, Priest, and King

Whether the members of the synod of 1791 were aware of it or not, their threefold structure reflected some very basic Reformation convictions about the doctrines of Christ and the church. All of the Reformed churches taught that our Lord Jesus Christ was anointed to a threefold office: he was prophet, priest, and king.[4]

This threefold office belongs not only to Christ, but also to every Christian with him. Each one of us is anointed to the threefold ministry of prophecy, of priesthood, and of royalty.[5] In the words of the Heidelberg Catechism (Answer 32), our prophecy is when we "confess Christ's name," our priesthood is when we "present ourselves as living sacrifices of thanks," and our royalty is when we "strive against sin and afterward reign with Christ."

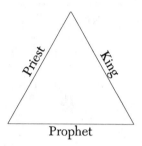

Prophet

The threefold ministry of individual believers is also shared by the church as a whole, since, as the congregation of the faithful, it is the collection into a single body of all Christian individuals.[6] The collective threefold ministry is revealed in 1 Peter 2:9, where the apostle calls the church a "royal priesthood and a holy nation," given the task to "declare the wonderful deeds of him who called you out of darkness into his marvelous light." Here are royalty, priesthood, and prophecy. Since the church is not merely a collection of individuals but even more the Body of Christ, the church maintains in a communal form Christ's personal offices of prophet, priest, and king.

We believe that the Lord Jesus Christ is very much alive, and always active in the church. Where Christ is active and his Lordship is honored and obeyed, that is the "true church." The true church has certain marks by which it may be known, and these marks are directly related to the threefold office of Christ who is active within it as prophet, priest, and king. The three "Marks of the True Church" are described by Article 29 of the Belgic Confession. They are, first, "the pure preaching of the gospel," second, "the pure administration of the sacraments," and third, "the practice of church discipline."

How are these marks of the church related to the threefold office of Christ? First, preaching arises out of the gift of prophecy.

It also relates to priesthood and to royalty, when it bears witness to Jesus' heavenly high-priesthood and his finished work for our salvation, and when it testifies to Christ's claims as king. Second, the administration of the sacraments arises out of Jesus' priestly work upon the cross, his prayer for us, and the communication to us of the benefits of his sacrifice by means of the washing in his blood and the breaking of the bread. But the sacraments are also prophetic, when they celebrate the promises of God as present realities that we can touch and taste and see. They are also royal prophecies when they point us to the celestial banquet, when, after having washed our robes in the blood of the lamb, we shall sit down for the royal feast, when his kingdom has fully come. Third, church discipline arises out of the rightful claims of Jesus' kingship. It also points to the holiness of his priestly work, to which we must come repentant and hungry, and it points to the power of his prophetic word, which cuts as sharp as any sword, revealing the secrets that are within the hearts of men and women and announcing the way of salvation.

We include these three marks of the church in our triangular diagram as "braces" running from the center of each leg to the opposite point. These braces give the triangle its shape, and they illustrate that, in fact, the "marks of the church" are what actually give the constitution its shape. They show God's actions that generate the church, while the triangle's legs are how the Reformed church has embodied those actions.

Doctrine

Each of these braces is grounded in one of the legs, and each supports the other two legs of the triangle. Thus, for example, while preaching arises out of doctrine, it takes place within worship and it gives direction to the church's government. The sacraments arise out of liturgy, but they confirm the word that is preached, and they actually create the congregation which is to be governed.

The basic Reformed theology that is reflected in the RCA Constitution came out of the Reformation's interpretation of the Bible. The early Reformed churches tried to put into practice (though not in slavish imitation) what they read in the New Testament about the apostolic church. So it ought to be the case that the RCA Constitution reflects the New Testament pattern of the church, even if the members of the 1791 synod were not consciously attending to this. It turns out that the shape of the RCA Constitution quite closely reflects the reconstitution of the church on the day of Pentecost, as we find it described in Acts 2:41-42:

> So those who received [Peter's] word were baptized, and there were added that day about three thousand souls. And they devoted themselves to the apostles' teaching and fellowship, to the breaking of bread and the prayers, [italics mine].

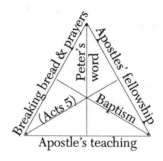

Apostle's teaching

Peter's word, his preaching, was the beginning action, so it is the central and upward brace. Baptism was the second action, and it is the second brace. Discipline was the third action, and, not unnaturally, it did not have to be practiced immediately but began in Acts 5, with Ananias and Sapphira. The apostles' teaching maintained what had begun, and it is the basic leg of doctrine. The apostles' fellowship also maintained what was begun, and that is the second leg, government. The breaking of bread and the *prayers* celebrated what was begun and also maintained it, and that is the third leg, liturgy. (Since the word *fellowship* can also be translated *communion* we could include that with the "bread and prayers.") The rest of the Book of the Acts shows how the apostles developed this primitive constitution in order to face the circumstances of expanding mission.

We see that the three-legged constitution of the Reformed church reflects the apostolic constitution of the Book of Acts. We should better say that it is an attempt to *obey* the apostolic constitution. We dare not say that it is the only way of obeying it, but it is the best way we know. If we are shown a better way, then, as an "evangelical church," under the authority of the scriptures, the RCA is bound to "reform" its constitution according to that better way.

The Acts 2 passage shows that there is a certain priority to preaching the word. That is why the Reformed churches called it the "first mark" of the true church. That is also one of the reasons why doctrine, or confession, is the basic leg of the triangle. Another reason is that, in Matthew 16:16-19, our Lord himself said he would build his church on Peter's confession. All the churches that came directly out of the Reformation, Lutheran as well as Reformed, regard doctrine or confession as the basic leg of the church. That is why we call these churches "confessional churches," the RCA included. To be a confessional church means that the church's being, its essence, its whole reason for existence, stands on its confession about God, its testimony to the world, its witness to Christ, its mission for the kingdom. The Reformed church cancels its right to exist if it fails to confess to the world in a way that can be understood by the world.

The Constitution and the Bible

There are "evangelical" churches which claim that they do not need a formal constitution, since the Bible is the "only rule of faith and practice." They will claim, for example, "no creed but Christ," or no "man-made liturgy,"[8] or no rules of church government to bind the freedom of the conscience or the work of the Spirit. The Reformed church also makes the claim that "the Holy

Scriptures are the only rule of faith and practice" in the denomination.[9] Why, then, does the Reformed church also expect its officers to obey the constitution, and its pastors to "preach the Catechism?"

To answer this question, it must be recognized that everyone reads the Bible with some pre-set ideas or expectations, and with some worldview already in place. No one can possibly come to the Bible completely fresh. To put it more strongly, we do not lose our biases and prejudices the minute we start reading the Bible. The culture we live in, our family backgrounds, the language we speak, all these things are the "flesh" that influences the way we interpret and apply the scripture. Common sense tells us that if a church has "no creed but Christ," then there is nothing to stop that church from finding in the Bible only those things that fit in to the prevailing worldview.

The Reformed church has a constitution just exactly for the purpose of being faithful to the Bible. The constitution is meant to be like the keel of a sailboat. The keel keeps the boat steady against the wind. The constitution keeps the Reformed church from being caught up and carried off course by whatever winds may be prevailing at the moment. The constitution is meant to do exactly what some people don't like about it: it is meant to restrict the freedom of individual interpretation of the Bible and to narrow the range of group application of the Bible.

The constitution is not meant to be a substitute for the Bible. It is meant to be an interpretation of the Bible and an application of the Bible. It is meant to help the Reformed church put the scriptures into practice, making use of the wisdom and experience of its tradition. For example, someone might ask what the Bible demands of our worship today. The answer to that question is provided by the Liturgy. The Liturgy contains precisely what the Reformed church believes the Bible is calling on it to do in worship. Or, what does the Bible demand of a church's organization? That's the Government. This also means, by implication, that whatever is not an application of the Bible really doesn't belong in the constitution. Other material can exist in other documents, like by-laws or policies or source-books, any of which can be changed without changing the church itself.

The constitution can be thought of as our common practical

commentary on the scriptures. Most commentaries deal with a particular book of the Bible, helping modern readers see what is really in that book and what's not. Such commentaries are not really concerned with putting the particular book of the Bible into practice. Application is up to the reader. The constitution is a commentary that works from the other direction. It starts from practice. It starts with the very practical questions, with the necessities of the ordinary life of God's people. It finds the answers to those questions in the Bible and puts it all together in a workable format. It doesn't ask the Greek and Hebrew questions; it leaves them to the specialists. It assumes that the church has the right to interpret the scriptures, and it also assumes that the church, on the whole, can know what it's talking about.

The Apostles Creed provides a good example of how the constitution interprets and applies the Bible. This creed is described by the Heidelberg Catechism as the "summary of the gospel promises."[10] What the creed does is take the gospel stories of both Testaments, boil them down, let the promises rise to the top, and collect them all together. Put another way, the Bible can be pictured as a newspaper. It has lots of stories in it, lots of facts and figures and statistics, and some of the statistics you won't remember from one day to the next (like the material in the Book of Numbers!). The Apostles Creed is all the headlines of that newspaper, cut out from each page and pasted one after the other. Such a collection of headlines would be a summary of the day's news. The Apostles Creed is the summary of the Good News.

The Liturgy is another example of how the constitution interprets and applies the scriptures. The Liturgy is the recipe that turns the ingredients of the Bible into bread. Bread is the staff of life, a very basic food, but no one can go into the fields and harvest bread. Bread is made of four ingredients which are even more basic; bread is made of wheat, water, salt, and yeast. These four ingredients have to be harvested and gathered in their natural state. In its natural state, wheat is not something anyone can live on. Human stomachs cannot adequately digest it. Something has to be done to wheat to make it edible. The result is bread.

So it is with the Bible. There's a lot of raw material in the Bible that has to do with worship, prayer, singing, washing, and eating. How do modern people put those things into practice in a modern way that is still faithful to the Bible? The Liturgy is the recipe. The constitution is the whole cookbook.

The Constitution is Authoritative

The constitution is an interpretation and application of the scriptures, but it is not just anybody's interpretation. It is our *joint* interpretation as a church, and that means that together we agree to interpret the scriptures in a particular way. Even more, it is an *authoritative* interpretation, and that means that when we "do church," we agree to be guided by the constitution's interpretation and application of scripture. We surrender something to the constitution. We allow ourselves to be taught by it, to be channeled by it, and to let our reading of the Bible be directed by it. That is quite a bit of authority to give to a set of human documents. Yet every time a pastor is ordained and signs the Declaration for Ministers, that is what's happening. That pastor is surrendering a part of herself to the constitution. Every time an elder or deacon is ordained, she promises to do the same thing. No one is forced to do this. (Fortunately, we live in free democracies with no established churches, as the 1793 preface pointed out, and it is a purely voluntary thing to put oneself under the authority of the RCA Constitution.) The constitution is our *common authoritative interpretation and application of the Bible.*

There is no doubt that the Reformed church's constitution has the effect of restricting the freedom of some of the people within the church. Pastors, for example, are not free to teach any doctrine. Consistories are not free to offer any kind of worship. Of course, it often happens that pastors and consistories do just that, because the church has no police! Each group is responsible to watch itself. If a consistory wants to allow its pastor to preach different doctrines, and as long as no one in the congregation files a formal complaint, it can go on indefinitely.

The only regular enforcement happens once a year, when the consistory has to answer the "Constitutional Questions" and report those answers to the classis. One question asks whether the consistory is satisfied that the pastor's preaching has met the standards of the constitution. If a consistory should report, for example, that its pastor is not preaching the catechism every four years, the classis receiving the report may initiate disciplinary proceedings. But the classes are unlikely to do such things, and usually they intervene only when the pastor and the consistory do not get along. And the only ones who can complain in any way about a pastor are the specific consistory and classis to which the pastor belongs, because in the Reformed church, the only people who can file a formal complaint about a particular situation are those who are directly involved. For example, if a consistory in New Jersey thinks that a preacher in California is preaching false doctrine, there is nothing it can do about it. If the preacher's consistory and classis are content with the situation, it will go on, and they will be left to their own consciences.

The Reformed church has maintained throughout its history a rather strict constitution, but it has also tolerated a wide latitude in practice. At times this tolerance has been criticized as nothing other than laxity, and the Christian Reformed church seceded over this very issue. Why even have the Doctrines and Liturgy if the Government will not enforce them? Perhaps the answer is that there is humility and charity mixed in with the laxity. There is also a basic love of freedom at work, together with the conviction that freedom needs room to try new things. So the RCA takes a "wait and see" attitude on many practices which are literal violations of the constitution.

Freedom is an important word. The preface of 1793 begins with the phrase, "In consequence of that liberty wherewith Christ hath made his people free...." The Reformed churches were born out of the Reformation's struggle for freedom from the Roman system. Still, the Reformation idea of freedom was very different from the modern idea of freedom. The modern idea of freedom in principle sets no limits on individual thought or action. The individual should be free to think or do or say whatever he or she pleases, so long as it doesn't injure another individual. By contrast, the Reformation idea of freedom is not centered on the individual but on the Word of God—the freedom of the Word of God. The reason the church needs freedom is because the Word of God has to be free; the Word needs room to do its work; and the rules and traditions of the church should not be allowed to confine the Word. The freedom of the Word requires the church to practice discipline, not only of its errant members, but discipline of itself as an institution. The practice of self-discipline is especially incumbent upon those people who have authority and power in the church. Unfortunately, too often the freedom that is demanded by modern Christians ends up as license for particular individuals to get their way.

Every church must find a way to balance form and freedom. There are different strategies for doing this. The constitution embodies the RCA's strategy, which is to have a stout backbone and a strong skeleton from which to hang the flexible nerves and muscles. The bones are hard, but it is their very hardness that allows for maximum movement from the muscles. It is the unchanging structure of the bones that gives direction, strength, and purpose to the flexibility of the body. The RCA's approach is inner hardness and outer movement, inner stiffness and outer flexibility. The constitution is a strategy for a firm set of essentials, with freedom for different applications.

There are other denominations, including some Reformed ones, which use a different strategy for form and freedom. Their strategy might be compared to a lobster's exoskeleton, which has a hard shell and a soft center. Freedom is preserved for the most important things, the great spiritual matters of faith, and form applies to the less important matters of organization and procedure, where a relatively strict observance of the regulations is expected. This strategy has been the general tendency, since the Westminster Assembly, of the Presbyterian churches.

A good example of this strategy is found in worship, which the Westminster Assembly considered to be so important that no formal or written liturgy should be imposed upon a pastor or congregation. As a result, the Westminster Directory for Worship is one huge suggestion. The Directory says, "When you pray, pray something like this," and then gives an example. But the Reformed church's Liturgy has always said, "When you pray, pray this," and it gives an actual prayer. The oldest parts of our Liturgy had almost no directions or "rubrics," but only those things that actually had to be read. The oldest forms in our Liturgy assumed that it didn't matter whether pastors stood on their heads when they prayed them; just pray them. They also assumed that pastors would use their heads and make such passing alterations in the prayers as circumstances required. Our newer liturgical forms now include an increasing number of rubrics which give precise directions for many doctrinally unessential details.

The Whole Constitution is Discipline

When the constitution is working as our *common authoritative application of the Bible*, it is serving to discipline us. The word *discipline* has developed a bad connotation because it is often connected only with punishment. Although church discipline certainly does deal with punishment and admonition, the word *discipline* has another meaning as well. Its more positive meaning shines through in the word *self-discipline*. This meaning has to do with self-control, with knowing how to channel one's energies and appetites in order to reach a specific goal. A person on a diet uses this kind of discipline, and so does an athlete preparing for the Olympics. Discipline may mean choosing to do certain things "the hard way," or it may mean saying no to certain things which are not bad in themselves. Discipline is expected of Christians, of course, because we are disciples.

The apostle Paul wrote to the church in Corinth, "All things are lawful, but not all things are helpful" (1 Corinthians 6:12). He meant that the church should not necessarily choose every option that is open to it, nor should it exercise every freedom granted it. Wisdom has to come into play. The collective wisdom of the Reformed church is in its constitution; it serves as our communal self-control. Everyone who bears an office in the RCA agrees to accept its discipline, and the church as a whole agrees to discipline itself and to be faithful to its Standards.

The Liturgy functions as discipline, for example, when, in spite of the pressure of strong opinions or outside marketing, it helps the local congregation avoid what is flashy for the sake of what is solid, to avoid the liturgical candy in order to offer the liturgical oats. To refer again to the triangle analogy, the "brace" of discipline holds up the "leg" of liturgy, and the pastor must take discipline into account when she plans the Sunday service. Modesty and chastity can be important liturgical ideals![11] The whole constitution is discipline in the way it calls the Reformed church to be serious and sober, to be certain of its divine calling, and to pay attention to its task. It is our freely chosen communal self-discipline.

The constitution is our mutual self-discipline. We do not have to equate it with divine revelation in order to give authority to it. We don't claim that no one can be a Christian who doesn't subscribe to our constitution. It is not the Word of God. Yet, because we are confident that it agrees with the Word of God, it is the yoke of discipleship we all carry together. We don't say that others have to carry this yoke, but we all say that together we will. In other words, without judging other denominations, this is how we within our own denomination will hold each other accountable.[12]

This kind of communal self-discipline has an unexpected benefit for pastors. It means that the pastors have the right to be judged *only* by the constitution. They have the right *not to be judged* on the basis of the many other things that occupy our thoughts. They may not be judged according to the latest issues, nor by what the majority of their parishioners believe about those issues. What pastors think about all the other issues that consume our conversation is their business. They may have the most unpopular views in the world on certain things, but they have to be kept free from the power of majority opinion. The constitution is their protection. Pastors are in the public eye, and people in the public eye usually suffer from constant judgment on an endless number of small matters. These can wear a pastor down. By having a constitution, the church disciplines itself in the way it judges the people who serve it. By having a constitution to which the pastors are accountable, the Reformed church actually enhances the freedom of the Word!

The Whole Constitution is Confessional and Catechetical

The Reformed church is a confessional church. The basic leg of our triangle is confession, and this gives a predominantly

confessional character to the rest of the structure. The whole
constitution is confessional in three different ways: it testifies to
scripture, it testifies to the larger Church Catholic, and it testifies
to the world. We have already discussed that it testifies to
scripture and helps us interpret and apply the Word of God in
practical terms. But the constitution also testifies to scripture in
another way, by being the testimony to us of earlier generations.
It tells us how they have heard scripture and tried to live
accordingly. We are reminded of these forebears every time an
RCA pastor is welcomed into a new classis, when the Declaration
for Ministers is read, "I accept the *Standards* as historic and
faithful witnesses to the Word of God." The Belgic Confession,
for example, is an inspiring reminder of the testimony to God's
Word for which Guido De Brés was willing to give his life. The
liturgical forms, too, are full of testimonies about God.

Second, the whole constitution may be understood as the
Reformed church's corporate confession and testimony to the
Church Catholic. In fact, the very name "Reformed church"
means, "The Holy Catholic Church as Reformed according to the
Word of God." The constitution is how the Reformed church says
to the other churches, "We believe that the Bible is calling us to
preach and teach this way; we believe that the Bible is calling us
to worship this way; and we believe that the Bible is calling us to
be organized this way." And what we believe, that we must
confess, as we are taught by Romans 10:10. Echoing this, the
Belgic Confession opens with the words, "We believe with the
heart and confess with the mouth...."

Third, the constitution functions to help us testify to the whole
world. This was admirably expressed in the preface of 1793
(chapter 5) which was written with an eye not only to the other
churches, but also to the whole nation. The Reformed churches
have always believed that the kingdom of God is something much
larger than the church. All aspects of culture are within the realm
and rule of the risen Christ, including politics and economics, the
arts and sciences, everything. That means that the church's
confession is also directed to the wider culture. Article 36 of the
Belgic Confession makes some very strong statements about the
role of civil government. One could wish that the Reformed
church might have testified just as strongly on other aspects of

human culture.[13]

The whole constitution is also "catechetical." This means that the whole document aims to teach, every line of it, not just the Heidelberg Catechism within it. The whole thing means to teach us how to live out of the scriptures. It means to teach us the anatomy of the Body of Christ.

The generally catechetical nature of the constitution comes through very clearly in the Liturgy, especially the older forms within it. The liturgical forms we inherited from the Synod of Dort were often criticized for being too didactic, but the Netherlands Liturgy was designed specifically to be strong in teaching. It tended to focus on the evangelical promises more than the doxological mysteries. It tended to go deep rather than lofty, aiming for the "comfort" of the soul rather than the inspiration of the spirit. Its whole purpose was to teach the people how to live in comfort and die in peace. It was a catechetical liturgy.

The whole constitution is catechetical in that it teaches pastors, elders, and deacons how to serve the church. The constitution is a "How-to-be-a-Reformed-Church Kit" for modern consistories.[14] In an age when so much is expected of pastors, it helps them focus their ministries. And when so little is expected of elders and deacons, it helps them learn their ministries. It helps consistories know what is expected of them, and how to measure their congregations.

The congregations of the Reformed church deserve to have their consistories know and understand this practical catechism for running a church. The consistories deserve to have a constitution that can teach them, assist them, and even discipline them in their ministries. May this book help pastors, elders, deacons, and other leaders as well understand and appreciate their historic "How-to-be-a-Reformed-Church Kit."

VIII
The Constitution
in the Future:
Some Observations

"The Glue that Holds Us Together"

During the 1980s, the leaders of the Reformed church began asking the question, "What is the glue that holds us together?" This question has come out of the feeling that the Reformed Church in America is an increasingly diverse denomination. Its diversity is something to be celebrated, no one questions that, but one of the consequences of its diversity is that fewer and fewer common assumptions and habits can be taken for granted. In the second chapter we called these common assumptions and habits the "unwritten constitution." The unwritten constitution of the Reformed church was in many ways the "glue" that held us together, much like the unwritten constitutions of Canada and Great Britain, which are still holding those countries together.

But in 1993, in the Reformed church, just as in the nation of Canada, the glue is felt to be weakening. The result is that the members of the denomination are less loyal to it than they used to be. It is less "family." Members are no longer as likely to support denominational programs and mission efforts just because they're RCA. They are just as likely to support programs and mission efforts that have nothing to do with the RCA. It is often the case today that RCA members are RCA members only because the congregation they belong to just happens to be part of the RCA. Many members are not so much "Reformed" as generically Protestant. Their loyalty is not to the denomination but to the local congregation. When these members move elsewhere, they are just as likely to join some other denomination.

Quite obviously, for most of the RCA's history, its "unwritten constitution" was provided in great measure by its Dutch-American ethnicity. Even though the Reformed church was never exclusively Dutch, and even though in 1793 the denomination was worshiping in four different languages, still the Dutch-Americans were the predominant group. But the Dutch glue was by no means unbreakable. The RCA has suffered two secessions, and each one was a break between Dutchmen, not between the Dutch and some other group. The secession of the True Dutch Reformed church in the 1820s and the secession of the Christian Reformed church in the 1850s both suggest that the Dutch heritage itself was not really the glue that held the RCA together. In fact, in both secessions, the minority non-Dutch elements tended to be loyal to the denomination.

It is difficult to determine just what, during the last few decades, has been defining the unwritten constitution of the RCA. Recent demographic studies reported in the *Church Herald* have suggested that the non-Dutch elements are now the majority; less than half of the denomination's membership claims Dutch descent. There is no common underlying RCA culture that differs in any real way from the generally accepted culture of the United States and Canada. There is no distinct unwritten constitution. So what is the glue that holds us together?

Legally speaking, the only glue that has ever really held us together is the written constitution. This was true even in those times when there was a functioning unwritten constitution. It was true in the 1790s, when the denomination was still strongly Dutch. During those years, when the Reformed church's leaders could see that their familiar Dutch-American culture was going through radical changes, the forging of a constitution was precisely their strategy to hold the church together. This bicentennial history is written from the point of view that the strategy of the 1790s offers some wisdom toward a strategy for the 1990s. When the unwritten constitution no longer works, all that's left is the written one, and maybe that's as it should be.

For a long time the RCA has under-emphasized the importance of its written constitution. It is the rare RCA pastor who regularly preaches the Heidelberg Catechism, much less regularly studies the Belgic Confession for his or her own edification. Everyone knows that if the Canons of Dort were to be written today, they would never win the two-thirds vote necessary to be added to the constitution. No one would suggest that new people join the Reformed church because they are attracted by its use of the Belgic Confession, or because the RCA Liturgy offers things they can't get anywhere else. The RCA, like many other Protestant denominations, counts for its growth on the attractiveness of its local congregations and the appeal of its local pastors. It downplays its distinctive doctrines and liturgies. When it depends on purely local initiatives, this can have no effect but to cause a decline in denominational loyalty.

There is one exception. The Heidelberg Catechism appears to have enjoyed something of a small revival in the Reformed church. (This may be due as much to the influence of the *Bible Way* curriculum as anything else.) This is an example of the constitution actually working in the way it's supposed to work, as a living document that has authority because it is being used. It is building, feeding, and "forming" the church. In this case, the Heidelberg Catechism is "constituting" some part of the educational experience of a number of RCA Christians. And all those who have experienced the catechism, who have had their faith shaped by it in some way, have been bound together by a catechetical kind of glue. This living function of the catechism is the primary and most important way that a church's constitution is supposed to work. Only secondarily is the catechism meant to be a "law" for the church in the sense of a standard by which to judge somebody's orthodoxy. The example of the 1790s would advise the modern RCA to look for its glue in the various "living" documents, whether doctrinal, liturgical, or governmental, which can adequately and positively shape and form individual Christians and local congregations.

One very good example of a denomination where this is being done is the United Methodist church. In 1989 this denomination published its new *United Methodist Hymnal*, which is having tremendous success.[1] Included in this hymnal are seventy-seven pages of liturgical forms (including creeds) from the United Methodist Ritual. The Ritual does not have any "constitutional" status in the United Methodist church in the way that the Liturgy does in the RCA. No Methodist pastor is required to use any of them, even during the celebration of the sacraments. Yet, because these liturgical forms are so available and usable, they are *functioning* constitutionally; they are shaping and forming a whole generation of United Methodist believers.[2] Functionally speaking, they are even more constitutional than many parts of the RCA Constitution. But it is possible for the RCA Constitution to be put back to work.

It's obvious that this book has been written to advocate for the RCA Constitution. Speaking personally, I believe that it is one of the best things about the denomination. When a number of pastors from the United Church of Canada were considering coming into the Reformed church, I warned them, on one hand, that the Reformed church was facing the same issues as every other denomination, that it had many problems of its own, and that it had some habitual sins that perhaps the United church did not have. On the other hand, I also told them, with real conviction, that what the Reformed church had going for it was its constitution.

I also believe that the RCA Constitution needs some care. It needs pruning and weeding. Too many details have been incorporated over the years which are not properly "constitutional." These need to be culled out. The constitution needs to be tightened up and slimmed down, so that what remains can have real force. There is some wisdom in what Napoleon is supposed to have said, that "a constitution should be short and vague." It's not so much that the RCA Constitution needs to become more vague as it needs to be made more open. In many cases it prescribes too much, and too precisely. Many things ought to be left open to the interpretation of the respective consistories, classes, and synods. Other things ought to be interpreted by means of shorter-term policies, by-laws, and procedures that are not part of the constitution itself.

It is just because the Reformed church is increasingly diverse that the constitution needs to be streamlined and tightened up. Recently I was introducing the loose-leaf *Liturgy and Confessions* to a group of seminarians. One of them was an astute young pastor of an Asian congregation which had just joined the denomination. In some distress, he asked, "You mean that officially the Liturgy is *law* for the church? How can this be law for my congregation?" He pointed to some of the details in the newer Forms for Baptism and said that there was no way the culture of his people could incorporate these things into their worship.

One detail that he pointed out in particular was a rubric in the 1987 Baptism Form which prescribes, "*use Christian name, omit surname*." He asked, "What is a Christian name?" Of course, any good dictionary makes it quite clear that within the common English usage of North America, the term "Christian name" means the first name, or forename, as opposed to the surname or family name. But the meaning becomes less clear when one takes other cultures into account. Among Christians of Asian Indian background, for example, most people have two first names: an ethnically Indian name, such as *Susmita* or *Saroj*, and also a Western-sounding name, such as Stella or Angelina. The Western names, or "British names," are the ones they will refer to as their Christian names.[3] Surely it was not the intention of the rubric in the Form for Baptism to make a judgment against the use of non-Western names in baptism, but that might be the understanding in a congregation that had Asian Indian members. It is just such a cross-cultural situation that illustrates the problem of what is properly constitutional within a Reformed church. Our Doctrinal Standards do not teach a baptismal theology that requires the omission of the surname, nor is there anything else in the rest of the Constitution on the matter.[4] Does the Reformed church really want to make this a matter of our constitution? According to this example, does the constitution not try to prescribe too much? Isn't the result inevitable that the constitution will be ignored rather than obeyed and will be unable to function as a positive, living document?

Separating Constitution and Canons

An important first step that might be taken to streamline the constitution would be to separate out a great deal of the material that is now in it and relocate this material in a separate set of documents called the Canons. The constitution would contain the really fundamental material. The Canons would include important material that needs to retain status in the church, without being considered constitutional. In other words, this material can have authority, but it can also be changed without changing the Reformed church itself.

Such a development as this was already suggested to the General Synod of 1962:

> For several years the Committee on Revision of the Constitution has worked on the matter of rearranging the material of the Constitution into a better organized structure. Considerable progress has been made in this area. However, the committee is still of the opinion that the present constitution is improperly structured in that it contains elements which are properly constitution and other elements which are properly contained in By-laws. At the present time this reorganization is being made so as to separate the present material into two distinct sections: one, containing fundamental principles and another containing matters of procedure.[5]

A beginning was made by separating out the "Bylaws and Rules of Order of the General Synod," as we have it in the current *Book of Church Order*. But the reorganization could have gone much further.

The natural course would be to follow the lead of the Synod of Dort itself. In the years before 1619, there were many calls to rewrite sections of the Belgic Confession to make it stronger on the doctrine of predestination. The Synod of Dort decided against this course and left the confession as it substantially was. Rather, the synod composed its famous Canons. The Synod of Dort believed that the Belgic Confession was good enough as it was, but that certain *canons* were required which would be guides for correct interpretation and application. The term *canon* comes from the Greek word for a measuring stick, like a yardstick or a ruler. A canon is a ruler, or "rule," by which to measure whether one's "course" is "true."[6] The Canons of Dort were written as guides for the correct interpretation of the Belgic Confession, the catechism, and the scriptures. We would not be mistaken to describe the

Canons of Dort as a huge footnote to the Belgic Confession.

Using this example, a great many of the regulations in the present-day Government need to be separated out into a set of canons, because they are the practical interpretations and applications of the more fundamental principles which do belong in the constitution. For example, the procedures for forming union churches or for dissolving and transferring local congregations are hardly constitutional, they are properly canons. Similarly, the rule about the number of months that it takes for a theological student to prepare for a Certificate of Fitness for Ministry belongs to canons, not constitution. There are any number of other examples just like these. If such regulations were considered canons, they could be revised in the same manner as the Bylaws of Synod are revised, without having to go through the procedure of constitutional amendment. In practice, of course, the canons would have to be obeyed no less than the material in the constitution, but the different reasons *why* each would be obeyed would be clearer. What is in the constitution needs to be obeyed because it is the Reformed church's joint, authoritative interpretation of the Bible. What is in the canons needs to be obeyed because the General Synods have approved it as useful. That is quite a difference.

Notice that this proposal looks very much like a return to a separate set of explanatory articles. Indeed, if the original Explanatory Articles had not been included in the 1793 Constitution *per se*, they would have fit our description of canons quite well. The objection will then be raised that our forebears must have found this set-up inconvenient, or else why did they combine the two documents in 1833? It is a valid objection, but what was inconvenient for one era may be convenient for another. It was not always easy to coordinate the Explanatory Articles with the related articles in the Rules of Dort. But modern publishing techniques, even of the desk-top variety, offer quick and cheap ways to do this. Furthermore, in 1833 the Reformed church was as homogeneous and stable as it ever has been, before or since, and the General Synods had every reason to think that even the detailed regulations could be counted on to be as stable as any other parts of the constitution. That is no longer true.

The distinction between constitution and canons can be applied to the Doctrinal Standards. The Athanasian Creed is the first example of what should go in the canons; it is best regarded as a great footnote to the Nicene Creed. It is a creed for theologians, not for consistories. The second example is the Compendium, which few RCA members have ever seen, even though it has never officially been removed from the constitution. If it is to be retained, it belongs in the canons, or, in its place, there could be a modern successor. The most obvious example is the Canons of Dort. Whatever their virtues (and they are considerable, as anyone will discover who gives them a fair reading), they have long since ceased to function constitutionally. At best, we have condemned them to "benign neglect," which is not an attitude of integrity. If we put them with the rest of the canons, we might actually improve their status by beginning to regard them as a useful guide for Bible study, instead of a dark secret we want to deny. We might also add to our collection of canons such documents as the Belhar Confession of South Africa, as well as such a doctrinal statement as the RCA's *Our Song of Hope*, or the Christian Reformed church's initially more successful *Contemporary Testimony*.

The distinction between constitution and canon could be applied to the Liturgy. The Reformed church has long distinguished between two different kinds of liturgical forms, those which are "obligatory" forms and those which are "optional" or "specimen" forms. The obligatory forms would belong to the constitution, and the specimen forms, as well as the Directory, would belong to the canons. In the Communion Form, for example, the constitutional Liturgy might simply include the Creed, the Meaning of the Sacrament, and the full Eucharistic Prayer, including the Institution, the Lord's Prayer, and the "taking, blessing, breaking, and giving." If these eucharistic essentials were observed carefully and used faithfully, with the assumption that extraordinary celebrations might call for extemporaneous alterations, the whole rest of the Communion celebration could be improvised, making use of the canonical specimens or not. No matter which of the available alternative Communion forms were being used, the core elements would be shared by all congregations, no matter what their culture or worship style. From the Reformed point of view, what is fundamental to the "pure celebration of the sacraments" (the second mark of the church), is what gets prayed, not how somebody prays it.

There is a particular conviction about the true identity of the Reformed church behind the proposed division into constitution and canons. This is the conviction that the RCA is essentially the North American branch of a much larger, worldwide Reformed church. It is sometimes too easy for the Reformed church to think of itself as a completely independent religious organization with its own unique way of doing things. No one intends to do this, but, as Canadians will tell you, American institutions seem habitually unaware of the rest of the world. The Reformed church cannot think this way. To begin with, the RCA is an international denomination (very few denominations straddle the U.S.-Canadian border). But more than that, it confesses "One Holy Catholic and Apostolic Church," and it belongs to one of the great worldwide branches of Christianity. Speaking globally, the Reformed church is a worldwide fellowship of many indigenous churches which reflect their own nations and cultures. The worldwide Reformed church is no monolithic organization like the Roman Catholic church, nor is it even self-consciously unified like the Anglican Communion. It is perhaps more like the Eastern Orthodox church, which is a fellowship of legally independent ("autocephalous") bodies all sharing essentially the same doctrines, liturgy, and form of government. Of course, the individual Reformed bodies show much more variety than do the individual Orthodox bodies, but that variety in itself is a matter of theological conviction. If the Reformed Church in America begins to see itself as the local North American expression of a worldwide movement, then there is even more reason to reserve for its constitution those fundamental matters which might have worldwide validity, and to leave to a collection of canons those matters that have a narrower application.

A Hardcover Constitution Again

Once the present-day constitution is divided up into constitution and canons, the constitution is likely to be much more stable and unchanging. It would become feasible to publish once again a hard-cover *Constitution of the Reformed Church*. This book could contain the Heidelberg Catechism, the Belgic Confession, the basic Liturgy, and the fundamental Rules of Government. This book would belong to every pastor and every consistory, and a copy could well be presented to every elder and deacon. Such a book would make an excellent gift for persons who have made profession of faith or who have joined a congregation by transfer. Such a book would be a tremendous asset in "forming" Reformed church congregations and giving them confidence in the denomination. Such a book could help develop appropriate denominational loyalty. Such a book, by virtue of its availability, would go far towards addressing the need which the Constitutional Revision Committee pointed to in its 1957 report to synod:

> [The Constitution] should be so organized as to provide for ready reference, and its provisions should be stated so clearly and completely that the most uninitiated may easily follow its guidance.[7]

Such a book ought to be handbook size, like *Robert's Rules of Order*. It ought to be both durable and handsome, and laid out just as cleanly and carefully as the *Liturgy and Psalter* was in 1968. The first edition ought to have an expected life-span of twenty years. As a supplementary volume to this, and for the use of pastors and consistory officers, the denomination could publish a book in loose-leaf format called the *Canons of the Reformed Church*.

Behind the proposal for a hardcover edition of a streamlined *Constitution* is the conviction that what binds us together most effectively is not common assumptions or even common feeling, but common work. It is the work that we do together that manufactures glue. The specific kind of work that the church does is believing, witnessing (confessing), worshiping, and church government.[8] The strongest glue has sweat mixed in. By providing its consistories and classes with a hardcover constitution, the denomination could both honor and support the real work that is done by those local bodies. Denominational loyalty would be enhanced on the horizontal level by strengthening the working identity of local bodies. This is perhaps more important than the vertical loyalty of the local bodies to the higher and more centralized ones.

Further Implications for the Liturgy

A streamlined constitution would have a Liturgy that is much tighter, more flexible, and more inclusive. Instead of being a whole body, it would be a skeleton plus some of the major muscles. It would not prescribe the local body's complexion or hair color. It would include only those things that need to be said, from week to week and from celebration to celebration, those key items that would keep the local congregation both "evangelical" and "catholic," that is, true to the gospel of Jesus Christ in scripture, and true to the great tradition of the Holy Catholic Church. It would include only those things which would keep the local congregation building on the "foundation of the apostles."

Think again about the quandary of the young Asian pastor when he expressed his concern over the detailed rubrics in the Order of Baptism. When we examine the whole field of liturgy from a Reformed point of view, we can say that "the culture is in the rubrics." (Rubrics are the instructions and directions included within the liturgical text.) The Calvinistic churches, in spite of their great emphasis on doctrines and discipline, were all skimpy on liturgical rubrics, and they were also quick to adapt their liturgies to their specific national cultures. The fewer rubrics there are in a liturgy, the more adaptable it is and the more inclusive of many different cultures. In fact, except for their lengthiness, the portions of the RCA Liturgy which are the easiest to adapt for other cultures are the oldest forms. These have almost no rubrics. They contain little more than those things which have to be read or repeated out loud. The older forms consist of expositions (now called "Meaning of the Sacrament"), prayers, and vows. These are quite easily translated, and can be fit into celebrations that satisfy various cultures, especially since these prayers, vows, and expositions are so full of scriptural language. In fact, we have already mentioned (chapter 6) that the old Liturgy of 1793 was translated and published in Japanese, and in two languages of South India, Tamil and Telegu. Compared to what we have today, the old Liturgy was streamlined, and it was more adaptable to other cultures without having to be changed.

Changing the RCA Liturgy has always been a matter of constitutional amendment because of the underlying conviction that to change the Liturgy amounts to making a change in the church itself. For example, baptizing people a certain way, time after time, begins to form the congregation in that certain way. That this conviction is weakening in the RCA becomes apparent in the fact that the Liturgy, like the Government, is now published in the form of loose-leaf books. Of course, it is certainly useful for pastors to have a loose-leaf copy of the Liturgy and Confessions. But if the RCA wants its Liturgy to be functionally constitutional, it will have to do what the United Methodists have successfully done, that is, publish it in hardcover and make sure it gets into pew-racks and homes. The elders, deacons, teachers, and laity in general need a hardcover version that will serve as the functional constitution which forms the character of their faith.

The 1968 *Liturgy and Psalter* was a hardcover book, and in spite of its being out of date, its general attractiveness and usefulness led to a number of requests for its reprinting. In response, "the General Synod in 1989 ordered the reprinting of the liturgical forms in the 1968 *Liturgy and Psalms* [sic] and the 1987 *Worship the Lord*."[9] The Worship Commission stated that since "the creation and revision of liturgical forms is a continuous task in this area of rapidly-changing language norms and parish needs," it decided "to gather all the forms into a loose-leaf binder," so that "provisional and newly-approved forms can be added to the full collection."[10] The result is the bright red loose-leaf entitled *Liturgy and Confessions*.

The great virtue of this publication is that once again two thirds of the Constitution are available in a single source. But if a constitution is that which you can't change without changing yourself, the mere existence of the loose-leaf *Liturgy and Confessions* raises the question of whether the Liturgy, despite its legal status, can really *function* constitutionally. It has become a very complicated publication, with a great multitude of services. Because of the significant variety of alternative forms within it, the Liturgy cannot be said to contribute towards denominational unity. For example, there are as many as four remarkably different liturgical forms for the Sacrament of Baptism.[11] A congregation which uses the proposed 1990 form will, over time, develop an attitude to Baptism which will be very different from the attitude of a congregation which uses any one of the 1968 forms. By contrast, if one compares the various forms within the 1989 *United Methodist Hymnal* or the 1979 *Book of Common Prayer*, one finds that for each of the sacraments there is a basic underlying unity to all the alternative forms.

Practically speaking, the loose-leaf format of the *Liturgy and Confessions* in itself insures that the Liturgy cannot function constitutionally, because it will be a book for the church office, not for the parishioner's hand, and certainly not for the pew rack. Some congregations will undoubtedly reproduce portions of the Liturgy for inclusion in the weekly bulletin in an effort to give the Liturgy back to the people. But just because a congregation reads something out loud in unison does not mean that they have taken ownership of what they've read. The people are expected to say words that they themselves have not produced and have not had a chance to meditate on and make their own. The Liturgy has been given to their hands without it necessarily being given to their souls. This is especially so if the prayers and responses are changed from week to week. The congregations have little chance to incorporate the words.

The triangular structure of the constitution reminds us that Liturgy cannot be separated from Discipline and Doctrine. Truly to give the Liturgy to the people requires connecting it with the self-discipline of the pastors and the catechesis of the laity. The constitution must be a *functional* constitution no less than a *formal* constitution. Liturgical items need to be repeated again and again, they need to become familiar and dependable and to work their way into the collective memory of the congregation. The symbol of this is a hardcover book which invites disciplined use. The liturgical bulletins that are taken home end up being thrown out with the magazines and just as quickly forgotten. Might it not be better to have a hardcover liturgy that could have a place on the shelf next to the dictionary?

It is conceivable that the constitution could also be published in a devotional edition. This could include some of the canonical liturgical specimens, but also forms for morning and evening prayer, for individual and family devotions, for hospital and sickbed ministry, and a treasury of prayers (one of the real strengths of the 1968 *Liturgy and Psalter*). It might even include the lyrics (without music) of the psalms and hymns in the denominational hymnal, presented as a standard treasury of devotional poetry.[12] Such an edition could be most useful for private devotional life. It might also be useful for the pew-racks of those congregations that prefer the "American revival" style of church music. They would have the well-loved words of the standard hymns, and they would be able to use available tunes that would come closer to their own musical vernacular.

Discipline and Discipleship

The constitution has not been the living document that it might be. Is one reason for this that we have given too narrow a definition to Church Discipline? The "third mark of the church" has been understood as the exercise of church discipline "for correcting faults" (Belgic Confession 29). In this sense discipline has a purely judicial meaning. We have suggested that the idea of church discipline is really broader than just correction or punishment,[13] that it also includes the church's own communal self-control (see chapter 7). Could we not broaden it even further to include the whole life of discipleship?

When the Reformed church was an established church, to be a disciple of Christ was simply to be a good citizen with Christian morals. Now the Reformed church is a "free church," and no government claims to be Christian, so discipleship and citizenship are not automatically the same; they may even be in conflict. In Nazi Germany, when all the historic churches succumbed to the government, and when Bonhoeffer and others sat in prison, paying the cost of discipleship, didn't their discipleship become the most important "mark of the true church," more than the Word and the Sacraments, and even more than "discipline" traditionally understood?

The Reformed Church in America has been making efforts in the direction of discipleship. In 1980 the General Program Council initiated a program called Discovering Dynamic

Discipleship. This program did not get very far, perhaps just because it was a matter of program and not a fundamental matter of the constitution. There remains a "Division of Christian Discipleship" as a permanent program area, but there were never any changes contemplated in the skeleton of the church itself. For the Reformed church to develop discipleship as a distinguishing mark of the denomination, it will have to take some steps beyond its Reformation inheritance, as that inheritance is enshrined in the current constitution. There may be new thinking required about the ministry of the whole congregation, about the priesthood of believers, about the celebration of the sacraments and the practice of confirmation. The canons may have to include a new kind of Compendium, one that is designed not for children but for adults, and for their "whole life education."

When the constitution was published in 1793, the Reformed church was in the process of changing its understanding of how it was related to the outside world. In the Netherlands of the Synod of Dort, the Dutch Reformed church had been the established church, and it enjoyed the privileges and prerogatives that went with establishment. In North America, most of the Dutch Reformed congregations had had to make do without the privileges and prerogatives, and the 1793 constitution tried to convert that necessity into a virtue. In spite of this major difference, the Netherlands Synod of 1619 and the North American Synod of 1793 had this major thing in common: Christendom. The United States was assumed to be a genuinely Christian country, and generally a Protestant one. Although the Dutch church would have to share the field with other denominations, still, it could enjoy the support of the dominant culture of the nation, which was Protestant Christendom. The 1793 constitution was the mechanism which enabled the Dutch Reformed church to find its rightful place in American Christendom.

Two hundred years later, Christendom has lost its power in the United States and Canada. Even though the majority of North Americans define themselves as Christian, the really powerful institutions of their civilization, such as the civil government, the universities, and the multinational commercial corporations, are all decidedly "post-Christian." How shall the Reformed church relate to this kind of cultural environment? So far, the models for how the Reformed church relates to the outside world have come mostly from the Reformation. Now we might do better to look for our models in the experience of the early church, in the generations just after the apostles, surrounded as it was by the "pre-Christian" Hellenistic culture of the Roman Empire. It will be more and more the case that the very virtues which the culture blesses are the vices the church must discipline. Or, to put it positively, the church will have to propose to the world a radically different way of being truly human, and a truly alternative vision of the human community. Is discipleship perhaps the obvious model for this alternative way of being human in the world? And if the church is itself the congregation of God's humanity, will not therefore discipleship have to become one of the distinguishing marks of the true church, and will this not require that the RCA Constitution will have to be recast accordingly?

In Conclusion

The Reformed Church in America is one of those peculiar modern entities we call "denominations." That's not how it started out in 1628, but by 1793 that's what it had become. And it continues as such. It takes great pride in its claim that it is the oldest Protestant denomination with a continuous ministry in North America. But if we confess "the Holy Catholic Church," and if we recognize other denominations as being as valid as our own, and if we are generally committed to Christian unity, does the Reformed church really have the right to maintain its separate existence? For centuries the Reformed church has had ambiguous feelings about its existence, and it has made real efforts to merge with other denominations. Each one of these efforts has failed.[14]

From a Reformed point of view, what is a denomination's whole reason for being? Apart from fund drives and mission programs and "family" feelings, a denomination's peculiar service to the larger kingdom of God is that it serves as an accountability structure for congregations and ministers (including pastors, elders, deacons, and educators). Much of the other work that denominations do can be done just as well, sometimes even better, by Christian organizations that are not denominational. But only a denomination can be a structure of accountability for the officers of the church. The accountability structure of the RCA is two-dimensional: first, its ministers and its congregations are accountable to the constitution, and, second, its pastors and officers are accountable to groups of their peers, groups which are set up by the constitution. The real "program" agency of the denomination is the local ministry. The denomination serves a tremendous purpose in serving that local ministry and keeping it in a positive relationship with the larger Church Catholic. It keeps it accountable.

But accountability can take place in any denomination. Why keep this one going? Perhaps because these 900 or more congregations that are the Reformed church are also accountable to the larger Church Catholic. What they're accountable for is their particular tradition of doctrine, worship, and government. The Reformed church knows a particular way of being Christian together. As a confessional church, it is called to bear witness to the other churches and to the world. As long as it has a distinctive testimony to make, it may have the right to its continued existence as a denomination. If merging with some other group would put an end to that distinctive testimony, if an essential confession would be silenced, a confession that the Church Catholic in North America needs to keep hearing, then the RCA should maintain its existence. If it no longer has anything distinctive, however, then it really should not try to maintain its own independent structure of accountability.

The author of this book has had the privilege of bringing into his congregation's membership some twenty young adults over the past year. Not one of them had ever heard of the Reformed church. They have never been part of the RCA "family." The question arises, what identity should the pastor try to develop in such new members? Should the pastor first settle on some image of a "Reformed church member," and then work on helping these new members develop a conformity to that image? To whom must these new members belong? The obvious answer comes from the RCA Constitution itself. These new members "belong body and soul, life and death, to their faithful Savior Jesus Christ"

(Catechism Q 1) and therefore no one else, no other group, and no other family can have any claim on them. The only image to which they must conform is that of Christ himself (Ephesians 4), that they "may grow up in all things into him who is the Head, even Jesus Christ our Lord," as the 1968 Order for the Lord's Supper says. In this post-Christian era, we dare not give ourselves the agenda of trying to create loyal RCA members. If we do this, the church begins to make an idol of itself, looking for its future in the flesh, instead of by faith.

But one cannot make generic Christians. Even a discipleship that looks to first century models cannot ignore history. The Middle Ages happened, the Reformation happened, the Enlightenment happened, racism still happens. Disciples cannot be conformed to the image of Christ in a vacuum. They need to be formed in a way that relates to the culture in which they live. They need to be preached to, they need to be washed and fed with the sacraments, and they need to be governed. There have to be tools to do this. What the Reformed church has is tools. Isn't that what a denomination is, after all, a machine shop for the work of shaping disciples? The shop-workers are the pastors, elders, deacons, and educators, and the toolbox is the constitution.

In 1793 the Reformed church faced the question, "What is the glue that holds us together?" Today, with Christendom dying away, the Reformed church faces not only the same question but another that is more important, "What is our common business in God's world?" There is nothing to be afraid of; it is an exciting time of opportunity. May the constitution help the Reformed church to answer the questions it faces now no less than it did two hundred years ago.

Endnotes

Chapter I

1. It does not really mean "work of the people," despite what many scholars have written.
2. For the Belgic Confession and the Heidelberg Catechism, see Wilhelm Niesel, *Bekenntnisschriften und Kirchenordnungen der nach Gottes Wort reformierten Kirche*, 3rd ed., Zürich, 1938, pp. 119-218. A critical edition of the Canons of Dort has not been published, but the Latin original, in the *Acta Synodi Dordrechtanae*, is not rare. Good critical translations of the standards were produced by a series of synodical study committees of the Christian Reformed church. The Heidelberg Catechism was published in the 1975 *Acts of Synod*, the Belgic Confession in the 1983 *Acts of Synod*, and the Canons of Dort in the 1986 *Acts of Synod*. These are available in the booklet, *Ecumenical Creeds and Reformed Confessions*, continually published by CRC Publications. The RCA versions of these are available in the loose-leaf called *Liturgy and Con-fessions*, from the Reformed Church Press.
3. Daniel James Meeter, "The North American Liturgy: A critical edition of the Liturgy of the Reformed Dutch Church in North America, 1793," Diss., Drew University, 1989. Ann Arbor, University Microfilms #8921810.

Chapter II

1. See the United Church of Canada, *The Manual*, 27th revised edition (Toronto: The United Church Publishing House, 1989).
2. Glenn T. Miller, "Losing and Learning in Denominational Conflict," *The Christian Century*, 108:839-40, September 18-25, 1992. See also Bill J. Leonard, Pragmatic Compromise at Southern Seminary," *The Christian Century*, 108: 477-9, May 1, 1991, and Richard Leigh Walker, "Moderates Form

Alternative Fellowship," *Christianity Today*, 35:61, June 24, 1991.

3. "Therefore, we, (here insert the legal title of the church), hereby solemnly and in the fear of the Lord do call you, the said (N.N.) to be our pastor and teacher...in conformity with the Word of God and the *Constitution* of the Reformed Church in America, to which you, upon accepting this call, must, with us, remain subordinate." From the Call to a Minister in the Formu-laries of the Reformed Church in America, p. 104 in the *Book of Church Order*.

4. For a good history of the process see Edwin G. Mulder, "A Long Time in Coming," *Reformed Review*, 42:224-46, Spring, 1989.

5. *Minutes of the General Synod*, June 1979, p. 68.

6. William P. Brink and Richard R. De Ridder, *Manual of Christian Reformed Church Government*, 1979 edition (Grand Rapids: Board of Publications of the Christian Reformed Church, 1979), pp. 144-5, 190-2.

Chapter III

1. "No one whose testicles are crushed or whose penis is cut off shall be admitted to the assembly of the Lord." Philip found him reading Isaiah 53:7-8 in the chariot. The Isaiah passage is applied to Christ of course, but the author of Acts obviously intended that the passage should apply to the eunuch as well. The eunuch's second question (of three) suggests that he was drawn to it like to a mirror: "About whom, may I ask you, does the prophet say this, about himself or about someone else?"

2. Even after having learned this lesson, Peter succumbed to the temptation to deny it (Galatians 2:11-14).

3. Protestants should not throw the baby out with the bath water when it comes to this text. While it is true that the passage has nothing to do with the papacy, its focus on the particular person of Peter is too obvious to deny.

4. The Book of Exodus shows us how, by organizing the children of Israel, God solidified their freedom.

5. As taught by the Heidelberg Catechism:

    83. Q. What are the keys of the kingdom?
    A. The preaching of the holy gospel and Christian discipline. Both preaching and discipline open the kingdom of heaven to believers and close it to unbelievers.

    84. Q. How does preaching the gospel open and close the kingdom of heaven?
    A. According to the command of Christ: The kingdom of heaven is opened by proclaiming and publicly declaring to all believers, each and every one, that, as often as they accept the gospel promise in true faith, God, because of what Christ has done, truly forgives all their sins. The kingdom of heaven is closed, however, by proclaiming

and publicly declaring to unbelievers and hypocrites that, as long as they do not repent, the wrath of God and eternal condemnation rest on them. God's judgment, both in this life and in the life to come, is based on this gospel testimony.

6. *The First Apology of Justin, the Martyr.* Edward Rochie Hardy, ed. and trans., in Cyril C. Richardson, et al., ed., *Early Christian Fathers*, vol. I of *The Library of Christian Classics*, John Baillie, John T. McNeill, and Henry P. Van Dusen, ed. (Philadelphia: Westminster, 1953), p. 287.

7. Alexander Roberts and W. H. Rambaut, trans., *Irenaus: Against Heresies*, in the *Ante-Nicene Christian Library*, Alexander Roberts and James Donaldson, ed., vol. IX (Edinburgh, 1869), p. 11. At this stage bishops were still the pastors of congregations.

8. *The Teaching of the Twelve Apostles*, commonly called the *Didache*. Cyril C. Richardson, ed. and trans., in *Early Christian Fathers*, vol. I of *The Library of Christian Classics*, John Baillie, John T. McNeill, and Henry P. Van Dusen, ed. (Philadelphia: West-minster, 1953), pp. 161-182.

9. See "Apostolic Tradition," *Oxford Dictionary of the Christian Church*, 2nd ed., F. L. Cross and E. A. Livingstone, ed. (London, 1974), p. 76.

10. R. Hugh Connolly, *Didascalia Apostolorum: The Syriac Version Translated and Accompanied by the Verona Latin Fragments, with an Introduction and Notes* (Oxford, 1929). Its original title is "The Catholic Didascalia, that is, Teaching of the Twelve Holy Apostles and Disciples of our Saviour" or *Didascalia id est Doctrina catholica duodecim apostolorum et discipulorum sanctorum Saluatoris nostri* (Connolly, p. xxvii, p. 2). "The *Didascalia* is recognized on all hands as being a work of the third century, though opinion differs as to whether it is to be assigned to the first or the second half of the century.... The book has naturally been classed with that family of documents which we know as the Church Orders, among which it forms a third in point of time to the *Didache* and the *Apostolic Tradition* of Hippolytus." Connolly, pp. xxvi-xxvii.

11. *Constitutiones Sanctorum Aposto-lorum*, J.-P. Migne, *Patrologiæ Græcæ*, vol. I (Paris, 1857), p. 555. The Greek title is best translated as the "Ordinances of the Holy Apostles."

12. Connolly, *Didascalia*, p. xx.

13. James F. White, *Protestant Worship: Traditions in Transition* (Louisville: Westminster/John Knox Press, 1989), p. 67.

14. *La Forme des Prieres et Chantz Ecclesiastiques, avec la maniere d'administer les sacremens et consacrer le mariage selon la coustume de l'Eglise ancienne*, 1542. In Petrus Barth and Guilelmus Niesel, ed., *Joannis Calvini Opera*

Selecta, vol II, ed. Petrus Barth and Dora Scheuner (Munich: Chr. Kaiser, 1952), p. 11. See also Hughes Oliphant Old, *The Patristic Roots of Reformed Worship*, Zürcher Beiträge zur Reformations-geschichte (Zürich: Theologischer Verlag, 1975).

15. John T. McNeill, ed., Ford Lewis Battles, trans., *Calvin: Institutes of the Christian Religion*, vols. XX and XXI of *The Library of Christian Classics*, John Baillie, John T. McNeill, and Henry P. Van Dusen, ed. (Philadelphia: Westminster, 1953), IV,x,30, p. 1208.

Chapter IV

1. In those days, churches were "public" and schools were "private," the exact reverse of what we know today. The churches were expected to do what we expect our public schools to do, support the status quo and make good citizens. Modern culture puts education in the place where their culture put religion.

2. The Church Order of Dort was available in the *Kerkelyk Hant-boekje: Zeer dienstig en nodig voor Predikanten en Kerkenraden*. This little handbook of Dutch Reformed canon law was in the possession of most pastors and consistories. The handbook contained the texts of all the church orders, acts, and rulings of the earliest synods of the Dutch Reformed church, beginning with the 1568 Convent of Wezel. The handbook contained important rulings of subsequent provincial

synods to provide precedent for later cases. One very important section of the handbook was the text of the so-called *Post-Acta*. This is the minutes of the closing sessions of the 1619 Synod of Dort, when, after the more famous canons had been promulgated, and all the international delegates went home, the Dutch delegates stayed on to deal with more practical matters of church govern-ment and discipline.

3. The Synod of Dort had included the Formulae of Concord plus the Liturgy in its so-called "public documents."

4. The word *constitution* was used in 1738 in the Fundamental Articles of the Coetus. See *The Acts and Proceedings of the General Synod of the Reformed Protestant Dutch Church in North America. Vol. 1: Embracing the Period from 1771 to 1812, Preceded by the Minutes of the Coetus (1738-1754), and the Proceedings of the Conferentie (1755-1767), and Followed by the Minutes of the Original Particular Synod (1794-1799)*. (New York: 1859), p. vii. Hereafter *Acts of Synod*. Early uses of the phrase "Netherlandic Constitution" can be seen in *Ecclesiastical Records of the State of New York*, Seven Volumes (Albany, New York: 1901-1916), 6:3817, 4212. Hereafter *ERNY*.

5. For the history of the Reformed church in the colonial era, especially concerning the matter of its relations with the British government, see Gerald F. De Jong,

The Dutch Reformed Church in the American Colonies, The Historical Series of the Reformed Church in America, no. 5, edited by Donald J. Bruggink (Grand Rapids: Eerdmans, 1978), pp. 46-62. See also Randall Balmer, *A Perfect Babel of Confusion: Dutch Religion and English Culture in the Middle Colonies* (New York: Oxford, 1989).

6. For the history of the Coetus-Conferentie schism, see De Jong, *The Dutch Reformed Church in the American Colonies*, pp. 170-210.

7. *Acts of Synod*, 1:vii.

8. *ERNY*, 6:4212.

9. *ERNY*, 6:4235-36.

10. *ERNY*, 6:4242-48.

11. Between 1775 and 1784 only one letter reached Amsterdam from New York. See *ERNY*, 6:4305, 4311.

12. *ERNY*, 6:4312. Livingston added, "The common enemy to our religious liberties is now removed; and we have nothing to fear from the pride and domination of the Episcopal hierarchy." But the Presbyterians were still a cause of concern on the other side. Dominé Jacob Rutsen Hardenbergh wrote the following to Amsterdam in November, 1783: "There is among us a numerous and influential Denomination, known by the name of Presbyterians, who say that they were formerly connected with the established Church of Scotland, and, therefore, are essentially one with ours. For a considerable time, however, doubts have been springing up in the minds of many of our people concerning the

orthodoxy and the church-standing of these brethren. We know that the ancient Scotch church took care that no persons were admitted to the sacred ministry, unless they had previously declared that they held the Doctrine contained in their Confession of Faith and Catechism to be true, and thus in accord with the divinely Sacred Scriptures of the Old and New Testaments, and had entered also into the required engagement to conform themselves thereby in their teaching. These cautious principles the said Presbyterians have dispensed with and abandoned, each one of their Presbyteries or Classes being competent now to pass upon the fundamental teaching of their Church, and to admit, at pleasure, not only persons, but also their opinions. From this there has resulted among them a great difference in sentiment concerning several of the weightiest dogmas of Sacred Theology." *ERNY*, 6:4314.

13. For a review of the discussion see: John Pershing Luidens, "The Americanization of the Dutch Reformed Church" (Ph.D. dissertation, University of Oklahoma, 1969; Ann Arbor, MI: University Microfilms, n. d.), pp. 314-35.

14. See chapter 18, "Revolutionary Constitution Making 1775-1781," in Samuel Eliot Morison, *The Oxford History of the American People* (New York: Oxford, 1965), pp. 270-81.

15. Morison, *American People*, p. 304.

16. Morison, *American People*, pp. 305-15.

17. *Acts of Synod*, 1:141.

18. De Jong, *Church in Colonies*, pp. 224-25.

19. *Acts of Synod*, 1:185.

20. For Hardenbergh, Meyer, Romeyn, and Westerlo, see Edward Tanjore Corwin, *A Manual of the Reformed Church in America, 1628-1902*, 4th ed. (New York, 1902) pp. 511-14, 619-21, 683, 906-7. Hardenbergh was also a member of New Jersey's Constitutional Convention.

21. *Acts of Synod*, 1:201.

22. *Acts of Synod*, 1:210-11. Also to be included was the newly drafted "form of a call." *Acts of Synod*, 1:205. Undoubtedly the model for this, Church Order plus subsequent clarifications and rulings, was the *Kerkelyk Hantboekje*. We have no indication which Dutch text was used from which to make the translation, but we can presume that the members of the committee all had their *Hantboekjes*.

23. *Acts of Synod*, 1:218. This recommendation meant that the rulings of the particular synods after 1619 which were found in the *Hantboekje* and considered binding, would not be included.

24. See the "Preamble" in *The Book of Church Order: The Reformed Church in America*, 1987 edition (New York: Reformed Church Press, 1987), p. 1.

25. *Acts of Synod*, 1:218.

26. *Acts of Synod*, 1:218-19.

27. *Acts of Synod*, 1:226-27.

28. *Acts of Synod*, 1:229.

29. The synod also appointed Livingston to look after the psalmbook in the future. *Acts of Synod*, 1:236, 239.

30. It would appear that the author borrowed some of his language from the preface to the 1789 American *Book of Common Prayer*, but to a different end.

31. *Acts of Synod*, 1:245-46.

32. This terminology is adapted from Th. L. Haitjema's title, *De Nieuwere Geschiedenis van Neerlands Kerk der Hervorming: Van Gereformeerde Kerkstaat tot Christus-Belijdende Volkskerk*, (The Hague: Boekencentrum, 1964.) The Netherlands Reformed Church would not take similar steps for many years, and it suffered greatly in the meantime. Its Church Order was under the domain of the several provinces until 1795. The Napoleonic Revolution brought the church under the direct control of the national government, which kept control after the restoration of 1816. This was the chief cause of the Secession of 1834. When the secessionist leader Albertus Van Raalte came to the United States in 1846, he could advocate joining the North American branch of the church because it was still based substantially on the original Constitution of Dort. See Gerrit J. tenZythoff, *Sources of Secession: The Netherlands Hervormde Kerk on the Eve of the Dutch Immigration to the Midwest*, The Historical Series of the Reformed Church in America, no. 17, Donald J. Bruggink, ed. (Grand Rapids:

Eerdmans, 1987), pp. 35-39; and
Corwin, *Manual*, pp. 138-39.

33. *Acts of Synod*, 1:244.
34. Church Order of Dort, Art. 47-50,
    ERNY, 6:4222-23.
35. *Acts of Synod*, 1:257.

Chapter V

1. The full texts of the Confession and
   the canons as they appeared in the
   1793 Constitution are contained in
   Philip Schaff, *The Creeds of
   Christendom*, (New York, 1919) 3: 383-
   436, 581-97. The 1793 text of the
   catechism has not been printed since
   1863, when it was superseded by the
   Tercentennary Version, which,
   however, differs very little. See
   Schaff, *Creeds*, 1:536-40, 3:307-55. The
   Compendium is not avail-able in any
   modern Reformed church publication, even though the current *Book
   of Church Order* states that it belongs
   to the *Constitution* and *Doctrinal
   Standards*. For the text of the
   Liturgy as it was from the 1760s to
   the 1880s, see Meeter, "The North
   American Liturgy: a critical edition of
   the Liturgy of the Reformed Dutch
   Church in North America, 1793."
   Dissertation, Drew University, 1989.
   Ann Arbor, University Microfilms #
   8921810.

2. This is the spelling in the printed
   text.

3. The preface to the 1789 Prayer Book
   begins thus: "It is a most invaluable
   part of that blessed *liberty wherewith
   CHRIST hath made us free*, that in his

worship, different forms and usages
may without offence by allowed,
provided the substance of the Faith
be kept entire." The purpose of this
preface is to give an apology for the
numerous alterations made to the
1662 Prayer Book of the Church of
England. The Episcopal preface
points to the consequence of the
Revolution that "the different
religious denominations of
Christians in these States were left
at full and equal liberty to model
and organize their respective
Churches, and forms of worship,
and discipline, in such manner as
they might judge most convenient
for their future posterity; consis-
tently with the constitution and
laws of their country." The
concluding paragraph includes the
hope that "the whole will be
received and examined by every
true member of our Church, and
every sincere Christian, with a
meek, candid, and charitable frame
of mind; without prejudice or
prepossessions; seriously considering what Christianity is, and
what the truths of the Gospel
are...." The similarities of this
preface to the Reformed one, four
years later, are obvious. See Massey
Hamilton Shepherd Jr., *The Oxford
American Prayer Book Commentary*
(New York: Oxford, 1950), p. v.

4. Professor John Coakley of New
   Brunswick Seminary, who has been
   studying Livingston's life and
   theology, suggests the same in his
   soon to be published paper, "John

Henry Livingston and the Liberty of the Conscience," *Reformed Review*, winter 1992, p. 127. Livingston's doctoral dissertation at the University of Utrecht was on "The Sinai Covenant."

5. For an example of a Dutch provincial government enforcing prescribed written prayers for the pastor to read in the Sunday service see the *Groot Placaet-Boeck*, vols. 1-10 ('s-Graven-hage and Amsterdam, 1658-1797), 3:474-77.

6. See Daniel James Meeter, "The Puritan and Presbyterian Versions of the Netherlands Liturgy," *Nederlands Archief voor Kerk-geschiedenis*, (1990) 70-1:59-60.

7. This apparently, and curiously, ignores the Mennonites who had been settled in Pennsylvania for over a century. Perhaps, as Donald J. Bruggink has suggested privately, Living-ston distinguished in his own mind the peace-loving American Anabaptists from the more radical Anabaptists who were contemporary with the Belgic Confession.

8. In the Netherlands this included the *jus patronatus* inherited from the Middle Ages, which gave civil authorities the right of patronage, to nominate pastors to certain congrega-tions.

9. H. H. Kuyper, *De Post-Acta: Een Historische Studie* (Amsterdam, 1899), p. 246.

10. Corwin, *Digest*, p. 135.

11. Corwin, *Manual*, 4th ed., p. 128.

12. Corwin, *Digest*, p. 151.

13. This was the English metrical Psalter which was produced by the "Collegiate" Church in New York City. Its peculiar arrangement of tunes and lyrics had made it unpopular. See Meeter, "North American Liturgy," pp. 159-67.

14. See Meeter, "North American Liturgy," p. 84. John Coakley has pointed out that both Livingston and Laidlie had difficulties with the traditional Dutch observance of the "holy-days." See Alexander Gunn, *Memoirs of the Rev. John H. Livingston, D.D.S.T.P.* (New York, 1829), pp. 199-201.

15. See Meeter, "North American Liturgy," pp. 391, 420.

Chapter VI

1. See especially Eugene Heideman, "Theology," in James Van Hoeven, ed., *Piety and Patriotism: Bicen-tennial Studies of the Reformed Church in America, 1776-1976*. The Historical Series of the Reformed Church in America, no. 4, Donald J. Bruggink, gen. ed. (Grand Rapids, 1976), pp. 95-110. See also James W. Van Hoeven, "Dort and Albany: Reformed Theology Engages a New Culture," in his *Word and World: Reformed Theology in America*. The Historical Series of the Reformed Church in America, no. 16, Donald J. Bruggink, gen. ed. (Grand Rapids, 1986), pp. 16-19.

2. John Coakley, "John Henry Livingston and the Liberty of Conscience," *Reformed Review*, winter 1992, pp. 121-25.

3. Eugene Heideman, "It Made Us Who We Are," the *Church Herald*, December 1992, p. 8.
4. *The Book of Church Order*, p. 4.
5. Edward Tanjore Corwin, *A Digest of Constitutional and Synodical Legislation of the Reformed Church in America* (New York, 1906), p. 162.
6. Ibid.
7. The following editions of *The Constitution* can be found on the shelf in Sage Library at New Brunswick Seminary:

    (abbreviations: DS-Doctrinal Standards, L-Liturgy, CO-Church Order, GSR-General Synod Rules of Order, F-Formularies)

    1793-DS, L, CO
    1815-DS, L, CO, GSR
    1834-CO, F, GSR (new Church Order of 1833)
    1840-DS, L, CO, F, GSR
    1869-CO, F, GSR, plus Digest of Synodical Legislation
    1876-CO, F, GSR (new Church Order of 1874)
    1879-DS, L, CO, F, GSR
    1885-CO, F, GSR
    1892-CO, F, GSR
    1895-CO, F, GSR
    1901-CO, F, GSR
    1916-CO, F
    1920-CO, F
    1924-CO
    1930-CO, F
    1932-CO, F
    1939-CO, F
    1941-CO, F
    1957-CO (proposed, with report on Ordination of Women)
    1958-CO (proposed)
    1959-CO, F (annually thereafter, except 1960 and 1967)
    1968-G, F, GSR (annually thereafter, loose leaf in 1970)

    In 1968 the Church Order was wholly revised. There was a return to more accurate nomenclature. What had been known as the Church Order was now called "The Government," as in the 1793 Preface. What had come to be known as the *Constitution* was now called the *Book of Church Order*, including, as it did, the General Synod Rules of Order, which were not properly part of the constitution, and excluding fully two-thirds of it, the Standards and Liturgy, which, however, appeared in the same year in the *Liturgy and Psalter*. In the year 1968, the Reformed church possessed its full constitution in as decent a published form as it had enjoyed since 1879, but which form the church did not maintain.

8. Article 89, Section 4 reads as follows:
    "For the purpose of uniformity in the order of worship, the following is to be observed by all the churches:
    "1st. After a space for private devotion, the Minister shall introduce the public worship in the morning by invoking the Divine presence and blessing.
    "2d. Salutation.
    "3d. Reading the ten command-

ments, or some other portion of Scripture, or both.

"4th. Singing.

"5th. Prayer.

"6th. Singing.

"7th. Sermon.

"8th. Prayer.

"9th. Collection of Alms.

"10th. Singing.

"11th. Pronouncing the Apostolic Benediction.

"The order of the afternoon and evening services shall be the same as the morning, excepting the reading of the ten commandments. The last service on the Lord's day shall conclude with the Christian Doxology." Corwin, *Digest*, p. lxix.

9. Mildred W. Schuppert, *A Digest and Index of the Minutes of the General Synod of the Reformed Church in America: 1906-1957.* The Historical Series of the Reformed Church in America, no. 8, Donald J. Bruggink, gen. ed. (Grand Rapids, 1982), p. 56.

10. Ibid.

11. *MGS*, 1960, p. 122.

12. *MGS*, 1958, p. 139.

13. *MGS*, 1959, p. 246.

14. *MGS*, 1961, p. 128.

15. *MGS*, 1965, p. 160.

16. *MGS*, 1966, pp. 148, 165, 196-203, 267-71.

17. *MGS*, 1967, pp. 157, 169, 178-85, 203.

18. *MGS*, 1968, p. 169.

19. Schuppert, *Digest and Index*, p. 10.

20. Corwin, *Digest*, pp. 369-74. In 1906, E. T. Corwin reported that these changes had come in 1836, but they appeared already in Livingston's 1814 edition of the psalmbook: *The Psalms and Hymns, with the Catechism, Confession of Faith, and Liturgy of the Reformed Dutch Church in North America* (New York: George Forman, 1814). Livingston's actions and motives deserve further study, as does the silent acquiescence of the church. Corwin recognized that the changes were unauthorized, but he reflected his era's prejudices when he called them "a positive improvement," p. 370.

21. Corwin, *Digest*, pp. 681-82. The history of this critically important relationship remains unexamined.

22. *Acts of Synod*, 8:498.

23. See *The Doctrinal Standards and Liturgy of the Reformed Dutch Church*, rev. (Cape Town: J. H. Rose, 1876).

24. Arcot Mission of the Reformed Protestant Dutch Church in America, *The Liturgy of the Reformed Protestant Dutch Church in North America in Tamil*, Tamil Series, no. 5 (Madras: The American Mission Press, 1862).

25. *The Liturgy of the Reformed Church in America in Telugu*, fourth abridged edition (Madras: SPCK Press, 1891).

26. [Edward Rothsay Miller, trans.], *Liturgy of the Reformed Church in America in Japanese* (Tokyo: n.p., n.d.). "E. R. Miller" is handwritten on the title page. Miller went to Japan as a Reformed church missionary in 1872. He made a Japanese translation of the Heidelberg Catechism. Corwin, *Manual*, p. 630.

27. [George Schnucker, ed.], *Die Kirchenformulare der Reformierten Kirche in Amerika* (Cleveland: Central Publishing House, 1907). Copies of the four translations of the Liturgy are available in the Sage Library of the New Brunswick Theological Seminary. No doubt all four were made from the uncorrected received text, but this cannot be verified until these translations receive careful study.

28. Corwin, *Digest*, pp. 374-77.

29. Corwin, *Digest*, p. 377.

30. See *The Liturgy of the Reformed Church in America together with the Psalter Arranged for Responsive Reading* (New York: The Board of Publication of the Reformed Church in America, 1907), continually reprinted.

31. For which see *The Westminster Dictionary of Worship*, s.v. "Liturgical Movement, The," by H. Ellsworth Chandlee.

32. Richard C. Oudersluys, "Introduction," *A Companion to the Liturgy: A Guide to Worship in the Reformed Church in America*, Garrett C. Roorda, editor (New York: The Half Moon Press, 1971), p. V.

33. Gerrit T. Vander Lugt, ed., *The Liturgy of the Reformed Church in America together with the Psalter Selected and Arranged for Responsive Reading* (New York: The Board of Education, 1968), several times reprinted.

34. *Acts of Synod*, 1974:210. In 1962, six years before the appearance of the *Liturgy and Psalter*, the Committee on the Revision of the Liturgy became the *Permanent* Committee on the Revision of the Liturgy. The name change implies that the revision of the Liturgy is to be a never ending story. In 1974 the name was changed to the Worship Committee. See Mildred W. Schuppert, *A Digest and Index of the Minutes of the General Synod of the Reformed Church in America: 1958-1977*, The Historical Series of the Reformed Church in America, no. 7, Donald J. Bruggink, gen. ed. (Grand Rapids, 1979), p. 61.

35. James R. Esther and Donald J. Bruggink, eds. *Worship the Lord* (Grand Rapids, 1987), p. vii.

36. The Commission on Worship, "Introductory Note to the 1990 Edition," *Liturgy and Confessions* (n.p., Reformed Church Press, 1990), p. 1.

Chapter VII

1. The three ecumenical creeds are accepted by the whole Western church. They are the Apostles Creed, the Nicene Creed, and the Athanasian Creed. The Athanasian Creed serves to clarify the Nicene Creed. In the Constitution of 1793 the three ecumenical creeds were included as parts of the Liturgy, not as part of the Doctrinal Standards. The Apostles Creed appeared twice: in the Liturgy and in the Catechism.

The three Reformed confessions are the Belgic Confession, the

Heidelberg Catechism, and the Canons of the Synod of Dort. The canons were meant to clarify the Belgic Confession. The three confessions have also been called the "Forms of Unity" and the "Formulae of Concord."

2. The metrical Psalter was not included in the constitution, but it was assumed to be an important part of the Liturgy.

3. "Men geen liturgischen vinger kan geven zonder dat onmiddelijk de hele theologische hand wordt genomen." Gerardus van der Leeuw, *Liturgiek*, 2nd ed. (Nijkerk: Callenbach, 1946), p. 9.

4. The Reformed church teaches this doctrine in the Heidelberg Catechism, Question 31. One can sing this doctrine in the magnificent hymn by Isaac Watts, "Join All the Glorious Names," number 369 in *Rejoice in the Lord*.

5. Question 32 of the Catechism teaches this, making use of the fact that the word *Christian* literally means *little Christ*.

6. The threefold office of prophet, priest, and king is also applied to the ministry of pastors in the hymn by Denis Wortman, "God of the Prophets," number 429 in *Rejoice in the Lord*. Denis Wortman was a Reformed church pastor who wrote this hymn for the centennial of New Brunswick Theological Seminary.

7. The events of this passage are echoed in Question and Answer 65 of the Catechism: "Q. Since, then, faith alone makes us share in Christ and all

his blessings, where does that faith come from? A. The Holy Spirit creates it in our hearts by the preaching of the holy gospel, and confirms it by the use of the holy sacraments." See chapter 3 for a fuller discussion of this.

8. James F. White, *Protestant Worship: Traditions in Transition* (Louisville: Westminster/John Knox Press, 1989), pp. 119, 174.

9. The phrase is in the preamble to the *Government* in *The Book of Church Order*, p. 9.

10. Question and Answer 22.

11. Erik Routley, in his lectures, used the word "chastity" to describe Calvin's ideal for worship.

12. It was very early understood that the "Netherlandish Constitution," as a whole, was discipline. In 1645, the Dutch Reformed congregations in Great Britain published their version of it (remarkably similar to our own) in English, and the name they gave it was the *Corpus Disciplinae*, which means "The Body of Discipline." It included the Doctrines and Liturgy as well as the Church Order.

13. The Christian Reformed Church's new *Contemporary Testimony* goes a long way toward addressing the wider aspects of culture. The RCA's earlier attempt at such a testimony, *Our Song of Hope,* was never accepted as part of the Doctrinal Standards.

14. This terminology I first heard in an insightful (and very funny) lecture given on the Heidelberg Catechism

by the Rev. Dr. Arie Blok, pastor of the First Reformed Church of Chatham, Ontario. He said, "Now you know that the Heidelberg Catechism was originally part of the Palatinate Church Order of 1563, and that included rules for church government and administration as well as liturgical forms. Why did they do this? You have to understand that the Reformation spread quickly in the universities, where they all could read Latin, and it spread quickly in the cities among the merchants where they all could read German, but when it got out to the countryside, where the people couldn't read, the Reformation ground to a halt. And in the Palatinate, even as late as the 1560s, you had the reformer Ursinus in the University, and the reformer Olevianus in the Castle Church, but out in the countryside it was still Father Schultz and Father Schmidt. Now these were good people, but they weren't scholars. They didn't mind doing whatever they were told to do. So the Heidelberg Catechism is basically a "How-to-be-a-Protestant-minister Kit" for Father Schultz and Father Schmidt."

Transcribed by the author from Dr. Blok's lecture given April, 1989, at the All-Canada Leadership Conference of the Reformed Church, in Cambridge, Ontario.

Chapter VIII

1. *The United Methodist Hymnal: Book of United Methodist Worship* (Nashville, 1989). The liturgical forms it contains include the weekly Service of Word and Table (four forms), the Baptismal Covenant (four forms), a Service of Marriage, a Funeral Service, and Orders for Morning and Evening Prayer. There are also a good number of liturgical prayers.

2. The author is pastor of an ecumenical congregation which holds membership in both the Reformed and United Methodist denominations. The author's congregation has been using the *United Methodist Hymnal* for the last year with real satisfaction.

3. About half the membership of the author's congregation comes from the Indian state of Gujarat. The examples of the names which have been given belong to members of the author's Sunday bible class.

4. A. F. N. Lekkerkerker argues that from the Reformed point of view the parents and family are also the recipients of the baptism of a child. *Kanttekeningen bij het Hervormde Dienstboek*, vol. 2 ('s-Gravenhage: Boekencentrum, 1955), p. 55.

5. *MGS*, 1962, p. 140.

6. The Dutch word behind *canon* is *leerregel*, which signifies a measuring stick, or "rule," for doctrine.

7. *MGS*, 1957, p. 118.

8. Real worship is work much more than entertainment. A worship service is a business meeting with God.

9. The Commission on Worship,

"Introductory Note to the 1990 Edition," *Liturgy and Confessions* (n.p., Reformed Church Press, 1990), p. 1.

10. Ibid.

11. A new 1990 Order for Baptism is now in permissive use in the RCA, for eventual proposal as a constitutional amendment.

12. This is what Erik Routley had originally planned for *Rejoice in the Lord*. This kind of book would simply be a modern version of the old *R.P.D.C. Psalms and Hymns* of which every member of the denomination had a copy. The Evangelical churches (Reformed and Lutheran) in Germany all publish such books for their people, as does the Reformed church in Hungary.

13. The word "punishment" was used in the older translations of the Belgic Confession.

14. See Herman Harmelink III, *Ecumenism and the Reformed Church*, The Historical Series of the Reformed Church in America, no. 1, Donald J. Bruggink, gen. ed. (Grand Rapids, 1968).

Scripture Index

Exodus
19:6   19, 24

Deuteronomy
23:1   23

Psalms
118   21-2

Isaiah
53:7-8   194
66:1-2   22

Matthew
16:15-19   24-5, 164
18:15-18   89-90, 141
28:20   26

John
2:21   23
4:20   22
20:22   26

Acts
1:8   26
2   26
2:41-42   21, 29, 163
3:6   26
4:11   21
5   26, 163
5:12   21
6:42   22
7:55   22
8:1   22
8:4-25   22
8:26-39   23
10   24
11   24
11:19-21   22

Romans
10:10   172

Galatians
1:1   27
2:11-14   194

1 Corinthians
 3:11   25
 6:12   170
 12   108
 15:3-10   27

2 Corinthians
 5:20   26

Ephesians
 1:23   23
 2:19-22   23
 4   191
 4:11-12   27, 107

1 Timothy
 5:19   142

1 Peter
 2:4-6   23
 2:9   24, 161
 3   108

Revelation
 21:14   25

General Index

Adiaphora (things indifferent), 82, 94, 136

Amendment procedure, 144, 152

Anabaptists, 50, 53, 148, 202

Anglican (Episcopal) churches, 4, 32, 35, 106, 124, 198

Apostles Creed, 1, 7, 12, 166, 181, 208-9

Apostolic constitution, 21, 24-30, 163-4

Apostolic Constitutions, 28, 196

Apostolic Tradition, 28, 195

Appeals, 73, 118, 128, 131, 152

Athanasian Creed, 1, 7, 60, 181, 208-9

Baptism, 56, 59, 82-3, 119, 134-6, 146, 152, 178, 186, 212

Bassett, John, 144

Belgic Confession (Articles of Faith), 1, 6, 18, 32, 36, 41, 46, 49, 52-7, 81, 89, 100, 102-3, 106, 109, 161, 172, 176, 179, 183, 187, 192, 202-3, 212

Belhar Confession, 181

Bishops, 105-8, 185

Blok, Arie, 210-11

Bogermannus, Johannes, 95

Book of Church Order (*BCO*), 2, 154-5, 179, 203, 205, 210

Book of Common Prayer, 4, 51, 186, 200-2

Brink, William P., and Richard R. De Ridder, 193

British North America Act, 9, 14, 31

Bruggink, Donald J., 202

By-laws (Rules of Order) of General Synod, 2, 150, 154, 179-80

Call, Form of a, 57, 121-3, 193

Calvin, John, 29, 149, 196

Canada, constitution of, 9-10, 14, 37, 174

Candidates, 98-103, 125-9, 151

Canons, 178-83, 188, 212

Canons of Dort, 1, 6-7, 32, 41, 49, 51-2, 56, 60, 102-3, 109, 176, 179-81, 192, 203

Censura morum, 77

Chaplains, 64

Christian Reformed Church (CRC), 2, 12, 16-17, 69, 112, 144, 168, 175, 181, 192, 210

Christlicke Ordinancien (1554), 89

Church (christian) discipline, 56, 88-93, 121, 141-3, 187

208

Church-masters, 117
Church Order of 1578, 63
Church Order of 1586, 75
Church Order of 1619 (Rules of Dort),
  31-2, 36-44, 46, 61-96, 122, 180, 197
Classis of Albany, 15
Classis of Amsterdam, 31, 33-5, 44
Classis of Bergen, 15
Classis of Brooklyn, 15
Classis of Holland, 150
Classis of Mid-Hudson, 14
Classis of New Brunswick, 7, 15, 150
Classis of Raritan, 15
Coakley, John, 147, 202-4
Coetus and Conferentie, 33-4, 98, 197
Compendium, 7, 41, 46, 49, 52, 55, 58,
  150, 181, 188, 203
Confessional character, 41, 43, 51-2, 105-
  6, 164, 171-2
Confessions, 1, 39, 209
Congregational churches, 44, 117, 129
Consolation of the Sick, 56, 59, 155
Constitutional questions, 167
Contemporary Testimony (CRC), 181,
  210
Corpus Disciplinae, 210
Corwin, Edward Tanjore, 199, 203-4,
  206-7
Custom and practice, 15-16, 29

Dammon, Sebastianus, 95
Days of fasting, 86, 139
Deacons, 31, 57, 62, 65, 69-71, 75, 85, 92-
  3, 112-17, 122, 127, 189, 191
De Brés, Guido, 172
Declaration for Ministers, 100, 153,
  167, 172
DeJong, Gerald F., 198-9

Demarest, W. H. S., 3
Deputies, 77, 79-80, 126, 129, 152
Didache, 28, 195
Didascalia Apostolorum, 28, 195-6
Directory for Worship (RCA), 7, 158
Directory for Worship, Westminster,
  44, 169
Discipleship, 187-9, 191
Disciplinary Procedures, 1, 2, 7, 154,
  186
Discipline, 39, 41, 56-7, 96, 141, 152,
  170-1, 187, 210
Doctrinal Standards, 1, 2, 7, 39, 150,
  159, 172, 178, 203, 209-10
Doctrine, 39-41, 49, 159-60, 168
Dort, National Synod of (1619), 31, 33,
  37, 43, 49, 51-3, 61, 95-7, 143, 145, 148,
  179, 188
Durell, William, 41, 47

Ecumenical Creeds, 1, 192, 208
Elders, 57, 62, 69-71, 74-6, 78-9, 85, 92-
  3, 104, 112-17, 122, 124, 127-8, 132-3,
  135, 137, 142, 153, 189, 191
Emeritus ministers, 66, 104-5
Excommunication, 56, 59, 91-2, 119
Explanatory Articles, 40-1, 46, 49, 53,
  57, 96-144, 149, 151, 180

Faukelius, Hermannus, 52, 95
Feast days (holy days), 86-7, 139-40,
  152, 203
Flood Prayer, 146, 155-6
Formularies, 1, 100, 103, 111, 150, 193
Fræligh, Solomon, 144
Freedom, 94, 168-71
Fundamental Articles (1738), 33, 197
Funerals, 86, 140-41

General Program Council (GPC) 154, 187

General Synod Executive Committee, 154

German Reformed church, 44

God-parents, 82-3, 136, 152

Government, 1, 36, 39-45, 49, 96, 154-5, 159-60, 165, 180, 183, 210

Great Consistory, 116-7

Haitjema, Th. L., 200

Hardenbergh, Jacobus, 37, 198-200

Heidelbergh Catechism, 1, 6, 18, 21, 24, 32, 36, 41, 46, 49-52, 55, 58, 81, 87, 89, 99, 102-3, 109, 122, 134, 151, 161, 173-6, 179, 183, 191-2, 194-5, 209-10

Heideman, Eugene, 146, 148, 204

Hipppolytus, 28

Holy Catholic Church, 6, 18-19, 28, 172, 182, 184, 189

Hommius, Festus, 95

House-visitation (*huisbezoek*), 70, 137-8

Irenaeus of Lyon, 27, 29, 195

Japanese translation of the Liturgy, 156, 184, 207

Justin Martyr, 27, 29, 195

Kerkelyk Hantboekje, 39, 103, 197, 200

Kuyper, H. H., 203

Laidlie, Archibald, 36, 203

Leonard, Bill J., 193

Licensure, 98, 100, 126, 128

Linn, William, 41

Liturgy, 1-2, 4, 6, 13, 36, 39, 41, 44, 46, 49, 52, 56, 58-9, 150-60, 165-73, 176-8, 181-7, 192, 197, 203, 207, 209

Liturgy and Confessions, 2, 158, 177, 185-6, 192, 208, 212

Liturgy and Psalter, 157-8, 183, 185, 187, 205, 208

Livingston, John Henry, 34, 37, 40, 41-2, 51, 95, 108, 146-8, 198, 200, 202-4, 206

Locke, John, 147

Lord's supper, 56, 59, 84-5, 136-8, 119, 152

Magistrates, 50, 64, 66, 71-2, 75, 120, 142

Marks of the Church, 161-2, 164, 187

Matrimony, 59, 88, 119

Meeter, Daniel James, 192, 202-4

Meyer, Hermanus, 37, 108, 199

Michaelius, Jonas, 32

Miller, Glenn T., 193

Ministers, 57, 62-8, 74, 78-9, 81-3, 87, 92-3, 98-106, 119-29, 132-4, 137, 142, 152, 189-91

Missionaries, 65

Morison, Samuel Eliot, 199

Mulder, Edwin G., 193

Netherlandish Constitution, 32, 45, 53, 145, 160, 197-8, 210

Netherlands Reformed (*Hervormde*) Church, 2, 200

Nicene Creed, 1, 7, 13, 60, 181, 208-9

Order of worship, 152, 155-7, 205

Ordinations, 56, 59, 63, 67, 69-70, 103-4, 106, 113, 129

Our Song of Hope, 181, 210

Parochial schools, 69, 134

Patronage, 53, 64, 203

Post-Acta, 96, 103, 110, 112-3, 123, 134, 197

Presbyterian churches, 3, 32, 44, 53, 106, 147-8, 154, 169, 198-9, 202

Professorial certificate, 99, 111

Professors (doctors, teachers) of theology, 62, 68, 81-2, 99, 106-12, 130, 138

Prophet, priest, and king, 160-62

Provincial Synod of North Holland, 33-4, 130-1

Psalms (metrical) and hymns, 2, 32, 36, 51, 87-8, 138-9, 155, 203, 206, 209, 212

Puritanism, 53, 117, 140, 146-8, 202

Rejoice in the Lord, 157, 212

Reserve clause, 153

Rolandus, Jacobus, 95

Romeyn, Dirck, 37-8, 199

Rules of Government (1833), 77, 98, 117

Rules of Government (1874), 152

Rules of Government (1916), 152

Rules of Government (1959), 153

Rysdyck, Isaac, 95

Schoolmasters, 65, 68, 81, 133

Simon Peter, 24-27

Slaves (black people), 135-6, 152

Solemn inquiry, 119

South Africa, 33, 156, 181

Southern Baptist Convention, 12

Striker, Peter, 144

Subscription, 81, 99, 102-3, 109-10, 113, 126, 152-3

Synod (General) of 1581 (National Synod of Middelburgh), 86, 140

Synod (General) of 1619 (National Synod of Dort), 31, 33, 37, 43, 49, 51-3, 61, 95-7, 143, 145, 148, 179, 188

Synod (General) of 1794, 43

Synod (General) of 1819, 108

Synod (General) of 1833, 151

Synod (General) of 1885, 150

Synod (General) of 1889, 156

Synod (General) of 1918, 153

Synod (General) of 1950, 157

Synod (General) of 1959, 153

Synod (General) of 1961, 154

Synod (General) of 1962, 179

Synod (General) of 1965, 154

Synod (General) of 1967, 154

Synod (General) of 1970, 155

Synod (General) of 1974, 157

Synod (General) of 1989, 158

Synod of Wisel [*sic*] of 1568 (Convent of Wezel), 136, 197

Synod (Particular) of 1574 (Provincial of Dordrecht), 87, 140

Synod (Particular) of 1788, 36-7, 41

Synod (Particular) of 1789, 37, 88

Synod (Particular) of 1790, 37-9, 123

Synod (Particular) of 1791, special session, 38-9

Synod (Particular) of 1791, 39-40

Synod (Particular) of 1792, special session, 40, 42

Synod (Particular) of 1792, 41-2

Synod (Particular) of 1793, 41-3, 112, 188

Tamil and Telugu translations of the Liturgy, 156, 184, 207

True Dutch Reformed Church, 175

Union (convention, formula, Plan) of 1771/1772, 34-5, 37-8, 40, 95, 97, 143

United Church of Canada, 12, 177, 193

United Methodist Church, 176-7, 185-6, 211

United States Constitution, 2, 9, 11, 14, 17, 35, 40, 147

Van Hoeven, James, 146, 148, 204
Van Raalte, Albertus, 201
Visitors, 77, 127

Walker, Richard Leigh, 193
Walloon congregations, 80
Westerlo, Eilardus, 34, 37-8, 95, 123, 199
Westminster Assembly, 169
White, James F., 196, 210
Wilson, Peter, 41
Women's ordination, 13-17
Worship the Lord, 157-8, 185, 208